1942

Bell's Musical Publications

General Editor

ADRIAN . C . BOULT

Vera Effigies HENRICI PURCELL. Ætat: Suæ 24.

Portrait of Purcell by R. White.
From *Sonatas of Three Parts*.

HENRY PURCELL

The English Musical Tradition

BY

A. K. HOLLAND

> " And for this reason in every age ye musick
> of that time seems best, and they say, are wee
> not wonderfully Improved? and to comparing
> what they doe know with what they doe not
> know, they are as clear of opinion, as that
> they doubt nothing."
>
> THE HON. ROGER NORTH (1728)

LONDON

G. BELL AND SONS LTD

1932

*Printed in Great Britain by The Camelot Press Limited
London and Southampton*

CONTENTS

PART ONE

THE TIMES

CHAPTER I

ANTECEDENTS

UNTIL comparatively recent times, English musical history has been written almost exclusively from the angle of the great foreign schools. Preferable as this, no doubt, is to the task which French writers have so often set themselves, of relating every phase of the national music to a pure, home-bred tradition, the converse method of referring English music at every stage to the main tendencies elsewhere, whether in Italy, Germany or wherever the current seemed to be running most strongly at the moment, has its own peculiar disadvantages. For it has resulted that whenever English music has assumed a leading importance, our historians have been rather at a loss to explain its place in the general scheme of things. It would appear to the casual student of musical history that the erratic English genius has rarely been capable of doing the right thing, from the evolutionary point of view, at the right moment. Thus, judged by European standards, the famous 13th century round 'Sumer is icumen in' has seemed as premature as the

3

equally surprising Tudor madrigal school was belated. English music in these circumstances has worn the appearance of being an historical anomaly, a misfit, or a sport.[1] And the lack of continuity in our musical development has become a matter of pained surprise on the part of our own writers and of ridicule among foreigners.

It has been recognised, of course, even if rather late in the day, that this country has from time to time made certain more or less significant contributions to the general development of music. Indeed Mr. Gustav Holst once went so far as to risk the opinion that the decisive strokes of musical invention have usually been the work of Englishmen – for example, the device of counterpoint, the device of modern harmony (those 'wrong notes' which the Elizabethan composers loved and which so shocked good Dr. Burney in the 18th century) and the devices of atmosphere and dramatic characterisation, these last being the particular contribution of Purcell. But such brilliant explorations, if they are fairly assigned, have not sufficed to place us on the map of Europe. At the end of every chapter of English musical history we meet the fatal objection: further progress barred. Various attempts have been made to account for this

[1] The word 'sport' above is used, it need hardly be said, in the biological, not the athletic, sense. 'Dido and Aeneas' is almost invariably spoken of as 'Purcell's freak opera.'

4

puzzling phenomenon of an art that has had beginnings but no continuity. The anomaly has been ascribed by some to our succession of foreign rulers and to the incurable bias of our cultured and leisured classes who, as Thomas Morley observed at the close of the 16th century, 'highly esteem whatsoever cometh from beyond the seas, and especially from Italy, be it never so simple, contemning that which is done at home though it be never so excellent.' Others have cited the great obstructing genius of Handel as the force which diverted English music from its true course, and again our literary men have been blamed for their apathy towards the sister art. A French writer, the learned Romain Rolland, has attributed our failure to the reluctance of English patrons to give the musician his due – Charles II's promises, as we know, were fairer than his payments. More simply, it has been said that we have not produced the necessary geniuses. These explanations, it must be confessed, bear some faint resemblance to the six reasons given by the schoolboy why he should not be whipped for stealing the apples: they are individually plausible, but mutually conflicting. At the very least, they prove too much.

That the discontinuity of the English musical tradition is not quite so great as has been supposed, will perhaps become more apparent as

5

the systematic revaluation of the 17th century, which has only just begun, is proceeded with. It is safe to say that no period stands in more urgent need of such revaluation. At present the century which saw the rise of instrumental chamber music, of the solo cantata, of the modern choral and dramatic forms, and which in this country was summed up in most departments by the genius of Henry Purcell, labours under the dead-weight of the late Sir Hubert Parry's depressing verdict: 'musically, it is almost a blank.' It has been written off as a period of transition; indeed for nearly a hundred and fifty years English music would seem to have been in this chronic state of transition. Music is a transitional art, but English music has spent its time passing over from one No-man's Land to another – so, at least, we are to believe.

One of the chief articles of musical belief is that the English are an exclusively vocal race, and it follows that in a period which saw the birth of instrumental forms they must inevitably take a back seat. Thus Dr. E. H. Fellowes, in his epoch-making account of the English madrigal school, says that 'when the decay of the polyphonic type of music set in, and when, simultaneously, the rise of the great schools of instrumental composition was heralded, English music suddenly ceased to be in the front rank, nor has it ever regained the proud position which it then lost. In fact, just so long as instrumental composition occupied a subordinate position in the scheme of musical development, English musicians were found in the foremost place, but so soon as the relative position of vocal and instrumental music became reversed, the music of this country at that same moment ceased to occupy a position of the foremost importance.'[1] Once again, we are faced with one of those periodic, sudden collapses of English music which have so perplexed evolutionary historians. In vain has an eminent foreign scholar traced one of the earliest and most original schools of keyboard music to this country, and in vain was the English school of violists acknowledged throughout Europe, in the first quarter of the 17th century, to be the leading example.

The year 1600 has generally been regarded as a catastrophic one for the art of vocal polyphony in which the English admittedly shone. The date has been accepted, no doubt for convenience as well as for its picturesque appearance, as marking a cleavage between the old art of many-voiced choral music and the new art of solo singing. This *annus mirabilis* saw the birth of opera and with it the declamatory style known as recitative.

[1] 'The English Madrigal Composers' (Oxford University Press, 1921).

7

It gave, so we are to infer, a secular and personal turn to an art which had up to that time been predominantly religious and impersonal. In fact it did everything to render problematical the appearance, rather more than a century later, of the religious, polyphonic music of J. S. Bach.

Recent writers have probably gone too far, by way of reaction against the dogmatism of the history-books, in alleging that this famous revolution never took place, or at the most, that it was a revolution in name rather than in fact. The history of Italian music in the 17th century, a history largely concerned with opera and its side-issue, the cantata for solo voice, is sufficient proof that the little group of amateurs who met in the house of Count Bardi in Florence, round about the turn of the century, builded even better than they knew. The fact that the movement was founded on a delusion (that of resuscitating in a modern form the dramatic art of ancient Greece) does not invalidate its claim to have promoted developments which were presently to assume formidable proportions. Many movements, religious as well as secular, have been founded on equally pious delusions, but that has not prevented them from attaining world-wide significance. Nor does the fact that there were certain anticipations of the Florentine experiments, in the domain of sacred oratorio more than a hundred years before, deprive the creators of the New Music of the credit of exercising a vital influence on musical development. That the direction which opera was destined very soon to take differed materially from that which its originators proposed, and that a movement of professed literary ideals was quickly transformed into one in which the claims of music were extravagantly vaunted, is only in accordance with the natural tendency of revolutionary movements to lose sight of their founders' aims, as soon as the first stone has been laid. At the same time, it is certain that no artistic system is ever completely and suddenly disrupted by the fulminations of a little group of theorists, whose immediate achievements vary, as they did in the case of the Florentine circle, in inverse proportion to the violence of their manifestoes. If the Italian revolution was less sudden and drastic than has sometimes been represented, in England its repercussions were still more cautiously received, and no account of English music in the 17th century which treats its progress merely in terms of a failure to keep pace with the Italians can be anything but misleading.

For one thing, the English musicians of the time, with no talent for producing artistic revolutions or issuing manifestoes, and with a singular disregard for the aesthetic value of dates, seem to have attached no particular importance to the

9

year 1600. It is quite true that in this year
Robert Jones issued his 'First Book of Songs and
Ayres of foure parts with Tableture for the Lute.
So made that all the parts together, or either of
them severally may be sung to the Lute, Or-
pherian or Viol de Gambo,' and that in this matter he had been anticipated three years earlier by
John Dowland, the most celebrated lutanist of his
age, who had issued his first volume of songs, with
an exactly similar inscription, in 1597. The conservatism of the English is nowhere more apparent
than when, in the act of making the most far-
reaching changes, they must needs believe, or at
the least pretend, that they are merely conforming
to custom, and since vocal part-music was the
custom, a whole school of solo songs must be
ushered in under the imputation of being 'ayres
of foure parts.' No doubt they could be sung in
that way and were possibly so conceived, but their
real significance, in the hands of Dowland, who
was the most sought-after solo-singer of his day,
was that they opened the way to the single voice
with independent instrumental accompaniment.
Campion, a few years later, is able to throw away
all pretences, though guarding himself against the
inveterate prejudice towards part-singing. 'These
ayres,' he says, 'were for the most part framed at
first for one voice with the lute or viol; but upon
occasion they have since been filled with more

parts, which whoso please may use, who like not may leave. Yet do we daily observe that when any shall sing a treble to an instrument, the standers-by will be offering at an inward part out of their own nature; and true or false, out it must, though to the perverting of the whole harmony.' Late in life Dowland had occasion to complain of those critics who said that what he did was 'after the old manner' and of the 'young men, professors of the lute, who vaunt themselves, to the disparagement of such as have been before their time, that there never was the like of them.'

Dowland, despite his originality, showed himself curiously traditional in matters of theory when he translated a Latinised treatise on music, the 'Micrologus,' that had appeared nearly a hundred years before, and commended its author and his somewhat antiquated principles. Theoretical conservatism is, of course, not necessarily incompatible with practical adventurousness. But apart from the fact that they could be sung by the solo voice, the expressive devices of Dowland's songs were merely a development of those which were current in the works of the madrigal-writers – rhythmic subtlety, word-painting, and harmonic suggestion. There was nothing comparable in the practice of the English song-writers to the complete abandonment of musical structure, in an attempt to make music serve the ends of poetic

declamation, of the Italian innovators. For anything approaching that idea we have to wait till
the 'Ayres and Dialogues' of Henry Lawes half a
century later (if we except a few half-hearted
attempts to introduce the recitative style into the
masques and early 'operas') and by that time the
New Music was already a thing of the past.

Indeed, the year 1600 is a date of no significance
in English music. The 'Triumphs of Oriana,' the
most famous of all madrigal collections, appeared
in 1603, and the leading figures of the English
polyphonic school lived on well into the 17th century. William Byrd, 'our Phoenix,' published an
important volume of madrigals in 1611. Wilbye,
greatest of the madrigalists, lived till 1638 and
was still writing in 1614, while Tomkins survived
till 1656, though he appears to have published
nothing in this kind after 1622.[1] And meanwhile
over the entire period, the fantasies of the composers for viols were transferring the idiom of the
polyphonic writers to a new field and producing
an instrumental development, as to which Roger
North affirmed that 'forreigners themselves use to
owne that the English in the Instrumental and the
Italians in the vocall music excelled.'

For the moment, the one channel through which
the New Music percolated into England was that

---

[1] A collection of his church music was, however, published
posthumously, as late as 1668.

of the Masques. The Masques were not a new form of entertainment. They had been introduced in Henry VIII's time, and indeed earlier, but it was under the Stuarts that they reached the height of splendour, costliness and scenic extravagance. They were not essentially dramatic in principle and consequently the motive behind the Italian conception of recitative was in this case somewhat lacking. Nor did they bear any real resemblance to Italian opera. They were, in short, a pastiche of poetry, allegory, song, dialogue, dance and spectacle, in which the music was of rather less importance than the scenes, which were indeed magnificent. Written by the leading poets and composers of the day and designed by eminent artists and architects, such as Inigo Jones, they were the popular diversion of the courts and noble houses of the early 17th century.

Charles I, whatever his political shortcomings may have been, was no mean connoisseur of the arts. He sent his 'ingenious vertuoso,' Nicholas Laniere, into Italy to buy pictures for the royal collection. Laniere was a man of many parts, lutanist, singer, composer, scene-painter and designer all rolled into one, and it was he who, on the occasion of Ben Jonson's masque 'Lovers made men' in 1617 'composed a recitative which for many years went about from hand to hand, even after the Restauration and at last crept out wretchedly drest among Playford's collection in print. The King was exceedingly pleased with this pathetick song and caused Lanneare often to sing it, to a consort attendance while he stood next, with his hand upon his shoulder. This was the first of the Recitativo kind that ever graced the English language and hath bin little followed till the latter attempt in our theaters.' This 'nonpareil,' as the excellent and fanciful North calls it, by no means succeeded in creating an immediate revolution in the English taste for the more formal airs and songs. A musical amateur like Pepys, later in the century, might indeed dabble in the composition of 'recitative musique' (much to the profit of that fashionable charlatan, Mr. Berkenshaw) but the progress of the 'stilo recitativo' in this country was painfully slow. Sir William Davenant, the practical experimentalist and impresario of the early English pseudo-operas, could only lament, in his introduction to the 'Siege of Rhodes' (1656) that the recitative is 'unpractised here though of great reputation amongst other nations.' And Matthew Locke, Purcell's immediate predecessor, in his preface to 'Psyche, or the English Opera' (1675) declares that 'though Italy is the great academy of the world for music and this species of entertainment, yet as this piece was to be performed in England, he mixed it with interlocutions, as more proper to our genius,' adding in a footnote 'We have properly no national recitative.'[1] And notwithstanding the transcendent efforts of Purcell to supply the deficiency, recitative never in fact became fully acclimatised and has to this day remained an exotic whose baleful influence on English declamation may be traced through the oratorios of Handel.

Early in the 18th century, the egregious Thomas Clayton, who fondly supposed that an English operatic style could be produced by the simple process of transplanting the Italian methods lock, stock and barrel, makes the apologetic plea for his abortive music that 'being recitative it may not, at first, meet with that general acceptance, as is to be hoped for, from the audience being better acquainted with it.' It was a vain hope. Twenty years later Gay can still get a laugh in the prologue to the 'Beggar's Opera' when he makes the author of his rogues' comedy say: 'I hope I may be forgiven, that I have not made my Opera unnatural, like those in vogue; for I have no recitative.' Addison summed up the whole matter in the 'Spectator,' in terms that are still applicable: 'The Recitative music in every Language should be as Different as the Tone or accent of each

[1] 'Other nations bestow the name of opera only on such plays whereof every word is sung. But Experience hath taught us that our English genius will not rellish that perpetual singing.' 'Gentleman's Journal,' Jan. 1692.

Language; for otherwise what may properly express a Passion in one Language will not do it in another. Everyone that has been long in Italy knows very well that the Cadences in the Recitativo bear a remote affinity to the Tone of their voices in ordinary conversation; or to speak more properly, are only the Accents of their Language made more Musical and Tuneful. . . . For this reason the Italian artists cannot agree with our English musicians in admiring Purcell's compositions and thinking his Tunes so wonderfully adapted to the words, because both Nations do not always express the same Passions by the same sounds' – a genuine point, although somewhat amateurishly put. Addison concludes that English composers should not try to imitate Italian recitative but to comply with the speech-accents and rhythms of their own language.[1]

Milton's famous sonnet to his friend Mr. Henry Lawes has often been cited :

> Harry, whose tuneful and well-measured song
> First taught our English music how to span
> Words with just note and accent, not to scan
> With Midas ears, committing short and long.

Lawes, who enjoyed a reputation in his own generation that was exceeded only by that of Purcell in the next, has always been rather

[1] Burney notes that Dr. Arne (in 'Artaxerxes,' 1762), 'found an English audience that could even tolerate recitative.'

contemptuously treated by historians, notwithstanding Milton's panegyric, from the days of Dr.
Burney, whose candour forced him to assert that
he could see nothing in the work of Lawes to
justify the praise lavished on him by all the
contemporary poets whose verses he so industri-
ously set. Indeed, Burney somewhat slyly hints
that when poetry claims the hand of music in
marriage, it instinctively chooses the more modest
and unassuming type of partner, and anyhow that
the praise of literary men ought in itself to make
musicians suspicious. Milton's lines remain,
indeed, a little hard to accept quite literally.
Even allowing for the partiality of a friend, it is
incredible, when one remembers that he was the
son of a quite reputable composer and himself
an excellent musician, that he should have
wilfully ignored the work of the poet-composer
Campion and other forerunners of Lawes who
aimed at 'coupling words and notes lovingly
together.' But it is just possible that among the
throng of contemporary composers and by the
side of the earlier attempts to introduce the
declamatory style into England, the 'Ayres and
Dialogues' of Lawes may have appeared the first
real step towards a new method of word-setting,
and it is from this angle that we have to approach
him as one of the more significant of the predecessors of Purcell.

Lawes had been in his youth a pupil of Coper-
ario, who as plain John Cooper went to Italy at
the beginning of the century and came back so
full of Italian ideas that he must needs change his
name. It was from Cooper, no doubt, that
Lawes inherited an interest in the new Italian
developments in secular music. More particularly,
in his work we find traces of the influence of the
most widely practised genre of the 17th century,
the cantata for solo voice, in which the forms of
recitative and air met for the first time on something like terms of reconciliation. But whereas the
trend of the Italian cantata was all in the direction
of exalting the music at the expense of the poetry (the
words often being in the most execrable taste) the
literary sensibilities of Lawes were exceptionally
fastidious and his music is inclined to seem deferential to the point of occasional flatness.

The best poets of the time – and it was an age
in which English poetry was exceptionally rich in
lyrical verse – competed with each other for the
privilege of having their work set to music by
Lawes. No one, says one of them, questions the
verses set by Lawes. Dr. Burney, who seems to
have experienced great difficulty in saying a
single good word for the English music of this
period, went over a song by Lawes in Milton's
'Comus' with a blue pencil and found irregu-
larities in that very 'just accent' for which the

poet had praised him. And after underlining a number of supposed errors which seem to point to the fact that the learned doctor was extra-ordinarily deficient in the sense of musical as distinct from merely literary accentuation, he winds up with this crushing judgment: 'I should be glad, indeed, to be informed by the most exclusive admirers of old ditties what is the musical merit of this song ['Sweet Echo'] except insipid simplicity and its having been set for a single voice instead of being mangled by that many-headed monster, Madrigal.'

Lawes, if anyone, is indeed a transitional composer in his vocal style. Compared with the ayres of the lutanists his songs lack subtleties of rhythm, other than those that are brought about by a faithful adherence to the verbal stresses and a rather uneasy consciousness of the growing importance of the bar-accent. His most frequent and obvious device to secure freedom of expression is a blank half-beat at the beginning of the bar or an anticipation of the accent with a binding-over of the last note of the preceding bar. He sets the verses line by line and the shape of his music is usually dictated by the words. A number of his pieces taken together are apt to seem monoto-nous, so frequently do the same devices of delayed entry or anticipated accent occur. But at his best, his music has a certain air of gallantry and good breeding – Lawes represents the man of taste in English music. The organisation of his songs is elementary beside that of some of Purcell's finest elegies and dialogues and he never rises to any very impassioned utterance.[1] But his fine literary sense prevents him from ever descending to the bathos and tastelessness of some of his successors. That he did not achieve a perfect equipoise between the claims of music and poetry is as true of his simpler and more metrical songs as of his declamatory dialogues. But he seems to have clearly understood that the resources of the old modes were for the time being exhausted and to have accepted to the full the implications of the modern scales. Purcell, while he carried the methods of Lawes much further, was in some sense a more traditional composer. Indeed he looked over the head of Lawes in one direction as he turned in another to the as yet unperceived possibilities of the future.

Lawes has left us one little memento which shows his sense of humour. Nothing is more amusing in the publications of this period than the valiant assertions of the composers and authors of prefaces as to the artistic independence of English music, coupled with their timid submission to the new tendencies of the age. The

[1] When he attempts it, as in the song, 'I prithee sweet to me be kind,' the famous 'just accent' is apt to go by the board.

20

instincts of the composers were, no doubt, inclined towards the maintenance of their native tradition, but the troubled times of the Civil Wars and the changing tastes of the public forced them to look for new departures. Lawes, with his training and experience, might have been expected to bow the knee to the Italians. In his preface to the 'Ayres and Dialogues' of 1653 he says 'I acknowledge the Italians the greatest Masters of Musick, but not all. And (without Depressing the Honour of other countries) I may say that our own Nation hath had and yet hath as able Musicians as any in Europe.' . . . As the second and the seventh are the most discordant notes in the scale, he continues, 'so to musicians a man's next Neighbour is farthest from him and none give forth so harsh a report of the English as the English themselves.' It was in this preface that Lawes tells the story of the joke he played on the dilettanti whose conceit it was to affect everything Italian. Taking an index of old Italian songs, he strung the titles together and set the whole nonsensical hotch-potch to music, giving out that it came from Italy 'whereby it passed for a rare Italian song.'[1]

[1] Tom d'Urfey in 'The English Stage Italianiz'd' (1726) was equally satirical. 'For the benefit of the English Quality and others who have forgot their Mother-Tongue This Play is translating into Italian by an Able Hand; and will be sold by the Orange-women and Door-Keepers at sixpence each, during the time of its performance.'

A man of stronger fibre, if less balanced temperament, than Lawes, was Matthew Locke. Apart from his significance as a composer, he deserves to rank as one of the most furious of pamphleteers in an age of furious pamphleteering. Like Purcell he worked in all the existing fields of church, stage, and chamber music. 'He was,' says Burney with his usual ruthlessness, 'the first that furnished our Stage with music in which a spark of genius is discoverable and who was indeed the best secular composer our country could boast till the time of Purcell.' That Locke was possessed of the spark of genius seems true enough. It was, indeed, a very fiery spark, and led to a good many explosions in the course of his explosive career. Probably the most forcible personality that has ever appeared in English music, he had a veritable passion for explaining himself and dumbfounded his enemies, real or supposed, with his terrific onslaughts. If not a literary genius like Berlioz, he has something of the same extravagant gift of expression. A head-long Rupert, he rushed into print on the smallest provocation and overwhelmed his opponents with extravagant abuse. As a musician he seems not to have quite known in what direction his true *métier* lay. He was at once an ardent champion of the old order and a protagonist of the new, a violent nationalist in theory and a student of

22

Italian methods in practice. He produced one of the latest works in the old style of consort viols and was Charles II's first composer for the violins, the 'upstart' instrument which was to 'put the viol out.' Conforming at last, as North tells us, to the modes of his time, he 'fell into the theatrical way and composed to the semi-operas divers pieces of vocal and instrumental entertainment, with very good success and then gave way to the Divine Purcell and others.'

We meet him first as a choir boy at Exeter where he has left a memorial of himself on the organ screen in the shape of his name 'Matthew Lock' carved boldly in letters two inches high; and not content with this, he repeated his exploit three years later, though on this occasion allowing his bare initials to suffice. The arrival of the Puritan forces led to the suppression of the Cathedral choir and in 1646, having learned as much as he could from his two masters (one of whom was Edward Gibbons, the brother of Orlando) the young man – he was not much more than sixteen – betook himself to London, where he added to his name the dignity of a final 'e.' Like most of the musicians of his time, Locke was a royalist – the Puritan hostility to church music was not calculated to endear them to members of the profession. So we find him a little later on some obscure errand in the Low Countries, where, as he tells us, he managed to copy a collection of songs by Flemish and Italian authors. Back in England, he collaborated with Christopher Gibbons in Shirley's Masque 'Cupid and Death' (1653) and three years later he arrives in print with the 'Little Consort of Three Parts: Containing Pavans, Ayres, Corants, Sarabands, for viols or violins ' – an accommodating style which shows the way the wind was blowing – designed for 'the Hands, Ears and Patience of young Beginners, making the Ayre familiar, the Parts formal, and all facile and short.' Locke does not let the occasion slip for a characteristic outburst. 'As for those Mountebanks of wit,' he says, 'who think it necessary to disparage all they meet with of their own Country-men's, because there have been and are some excellent things done by Strangers, I shall make bold to tell them (and I hope my known experience in this science will inforce them to confess me a competent Judge,) that I never yet saw any Forain Instrumental composition (a few French Corants excepted) worthy an English mans transcribing' – the transcriber of Italian airs is quite clear as to the English superiority in *instrumental* music. A few years afterwards, Pepys is to tell us (Diary, 21st February 1660) how he mét with Locke and Purcell (was it the father or the uncle of the composer ?) and 'with them to the Coffee House,' where they had 'variety of brave Italian and Spanish songs and a canon for eight voices which Mr. Lock had lately made on these words *Domine salvum fac Regem*' – the Restoration was in sight.

Henry Purcell the elder played with Locke in the 'Siege of Rhodes,' Davenant's experimental opera, in 1656. Locke's contribution, beyond the fact that he sang the part of the Admiral, consisted of the music to the fourth Act. As with the Masques, collaboration was a regular feature of those tentative works which, towards the close of the Commonwealth, crept uneasily on to the public stage under the cloak of music – English opera was brought into the world protesting its innocence. The music of the 'Siege of Rhodes' has never been found, but we get some idea of Locke's method in the music which he wrote for Shadwell's 'Psyche' and published, together with his instrumental music to 'The Tempest,' in 1675. As to the operatic form he says, in the preface, after claiming that something had been done ('and more by me than any other') to introduce opera into England, a work of this sort may justly wear the title of opera, 'though all the tragedy be not in musick,' for the author 'prudently considered' that the English talent did not lie in the same direction as that of the Italians. And then, with his inevitable truculence, he must anticipate the objections to which his music may give rise, such as 'The extream Compass of some of the parts. To which, the Idols of their own imagination may be pleas'd (if possible) to know, that he who composes for voices, not considering their extent, is like a Botching Stult, who being obliged to make Habits for men, cuts them out for Children. I suppose it needs no explication.' And furthermore, there are 'the extravagancies in some parts of the Composition, wherein (as among slender Grammarians) they may think fix'd rules are broken: but they may be satisfied, that whatever appears so, is only by way of Transition from Time or half-Time concords, and cover'd by the extream Parts: or to suspend the Ear and Judgment, for satisfying both in the Cadence.'

Locke is, perhaps, scarcely stretching a point when he claims to have done more than anyone to introduce opera to the English public, and it must be conceded to him that in point of dramatic technique he more than justifies Burney's tepid praise. Thus he writes 'A song of Echo's planted at distances within the scenes,' with the markings 'Lowd, soft, softer,' an anticipatory use of the double Echo which Purcell delighted to exploit, and incidentally one of the earliest examples of expression marks in English music. In the 'Tempest' he goes so far as to give the direction 'violent.' A more curious device is that of building

up a climax by increasing the number of parts,
one at a time. First the soprano voice enters solo
and is echoed, then the soprano and alto (echoed)
then soprano, alto and tenor, next the four parts
together and finally a 'chorus of all the voices and
instruments.' Some of his repetitions are faintly
comical, if typically operatic. Thus :

> Let us lowdly rejoice
> With glad heart and voice
> For the monster is dead
> And here is his head. (*bis*)
> For the monster is dead
> And here is his head.
> He's dead, he's dead,
> And here is his head.

This chorus is accompanied by kettledrums, wind-
instruments, violins, etc.

In sum, Locke shows a decidedly bold and
original genius. His style is angular and the
melody full of extravagant leaps, but his sense of
dramatic effect, though it may seem a trifle naïve
at this date, was in advance of anything that had
been achieved in England up to that time.[1] North
says of him that 'by the service and society of

[1] The question of the much disputed music to 'Macbeth'
traditionally assigned to Locke but also claimed as Purcell's,
has never been finally cleared up. There is a manuscript in
Purcell's handwriting, which proves nothing either as to its
authorship or the date of its composition. There is no reason to
suppose that, if Purcell wrote the music, he did so at the incre-
dibly early age of fourteen. See Mr. W. J. Lawrence's paper,
'Who wrote the famous "Macbeth" music?' ('Elizabethan
Playhouse,' etc. 1912).

forreigners' (he was in later life organist at the Catholic chapel of Somerset House, where Draghi and other Italians were employed) 'he was not a little Italianised,' though elsewhere he notes that the 'Italians did not approve of his manner of play but must be attended by more polite hands.'

Politeness was not, indeed, Matthew Locke's strong suit. After the Restoration, in 1660, he had composed the Coronation music for Charles II's triumphal progress to Westminster and having secured a place as composer for the violins, he entered on his career as a church musician. But it was not long before he managed to give offence to the more conservative members of the Chapel Royal. He ventured, in making a version of the Responses to the ten commandments, to introduce a different setting for each response. This unpardonable innovation roused the anger of the singers. The fat was in the fire and there was a disturbance. Locke rushed into print with a vindication of his music under the bombastic title of 'Modern Church Musick, Pre-accus'd Censur'd and Obstructed in its performance before his Majesty, April 1, 1666.' He is a slender observer of human action, he opens out, who finds not pride generally accompanied with ignorance and malice, what habit soever it wears. 'In my case zeal was its vizor, and innovation the crime.' It was not the fact, as had been alleged, that he was

guilty of startling novelties – were there not precedents in the excellent compositions of Mr. Tallis,
Mr. Byrd, and Mr. Gibbons, to say nothing of
later composers, his contemporaries? 'And to
speak rationally, should it be otherwise, art would
be no more art, composers useless, and science
pinnioned for destruction.' If he had contrived
to vary his little composition 'so as to conduct it
in the midway between the two extremes of gravity
and levity,' who would say that he was guilty,
except those whose proper place belonged in
Aesop's Manger? There had been a thing which
had lately 'crawled' into the world under the
notion that it was composition and had he the itch
for retaliation (which, of course, he had not, being
Matthew Locke) he might have something to say.
As it was, he left the matter in the hands of those
who were competent to judge.

Locke, in fact, is characteristic of the English
composers of his generation in his attempt to steer
a middle course during a period of change. A
bold experimenter in some directions, he is in
others curiously conservative. While foreshadow-
ing Purcell in his dramatic style, he was not able
to find his way in the new mode of church music.
Always ready to take credit for being an originator, he is at the same time the first to appeal to
tradition if challenged. Unlike Purcell, who is
said (though on the rather slender evidence of a

humorous catch) to have disliked the viols, Locke was among the last English composers to write for them. In the 'Present Practise of Musick Vindicated' he claims to understand the viols, but not to have the practical use of the lute, though he has composed several things for it, and in his 'Consort of ffoure parts' he attempts to make the best of the old world of the English fantasy and the new world of the instrumental suite. He wrote what was probably the first English treatise on the figured-bass,[1] but when the Reverend Thomas Salmon brought out his 'Essay to the Advancement of Musick by casting away the Perplexity of the different cliffs and writing all sorts of musick in one universal character,' Locke fell upon the unfortunate reformer, tooth and nail, with all the zeal of a defender of the traditional notation. Salmon's idea, which was not essentially impracticable, was to abolish the half-dozen or so clefs then in use, replacing them by a uniform stave in which the position of the notes would be

[1] 'Melothesia, or Certain General Rules for playing upon a Continued-Bass' (1673). Even in this modern text-book, Locke cannot avoid a tilt at the 'New Air-Mongers' who teach time and intervals only. 'These deluded mortals' (the pupils) he says, 'after all their Labour and Expence, remain as Compleatly Ignorant of what they've done, that when they come to hear any of their own Conceptions, they cunningly whisper their dear Pedagogue, "Master is this Mine?" After which, having received a gracious "affirmative Nod," they patiently retire; but with what content, I believe 'tis not hard to guess; they being thereby assured, they were as wise the first day they began, as at that instant.'

throughout constant, the different registers being indicated by letters representing Treble, Mean and Bass. Locke would have none of it, complaining, amid a good deal that was mere scurrility, that the Reverend Gentleman appeared to take the viol for a distressed lady and to fight for her relief, but instead had pinioned and fettered her to one key (which was not true), that he had left the organ and harpsichord 'emptier than three blue beans in a blown bladder' and had set the lute at defiance with her sister-instruments 'by buzzing in her head that she is supreme; which is as absolute a Tale of a Tub as ever wanted bottom or truth.' It is only fair to say that Salmon gave Locke as good as he had received in the way of acrimony. To Locke's scornful 'What will a man not do to be chronicled an inventor?' he replied with references to Billingsgate and the Bear-Garden, and likened Locke to 'a frightful scarecrow stuffed with straw, and furnished with an old hat and muckinger, holding forth his arms.' . . . Such were the controversial methods of the time.

The asperity of Locke's character, which the picture in the Oxford Music School helps to confirm, is a little softened by the glimpse we get of a kindlier nature in a letter that has been preserved. From his lodgings near the Savoy he sends a gracefully worded note round to his young friend,

Henry Purcell, who had lately been appointed copyist at the Abbey, beseeching him to join a little company of musicians the same evening, and to bring along his latest anthem and 'the canon we tried over together at our last meeting.' Purcell was just turned seventeen: Locke was a few years short of fifty and was soon to be succeeded by his young protégé as Composer in Ordinary for the Violin. Locke is not numbered among Purcell's official teachers, but it is clear that his association with the elder Purcell and with the uncle, Thomas, at the Chapel Royal, would bring him into contact with the family. Purcell repaid Locke's kindly interest with an Elegy on his death in 1677, in which the singularly affecting lines, shorn of the usual pseudo-classical symbols of the period with their weeping nymphs and shepherds, are set to music of touching and tender pathos.

Chapter II

THE RESTORATION SCENE

KING CHARLES II, riding up Whitehall to the sound of Matthew Locke's music for the sackbuts and cornets, must have felt that the needy days of his sojourn in France and the Low Countries had, at length, their compensations. His public reception had been entirely cordial. Mr. Locke's music had mingled pleasantly with the acclamations of the crowd and he had already marked out Mr. Locke for a new place as composer for the violins. The English were, doubtless, a trifle solemn and heavy in their musical tastes. But he was going to change all that. King Louis, whose tastes he so much admired, had a band of twenty-four violins. He, too, would have a band of twenty-four violins. Mr. Lawes, it appeared, had written the Coronation Anthem 'Zadok the Priest,' and having lost his fortunes during the troubles, with those of his Master (of ever blessed memory) had already been rewarded with a post in the Private Musick as composer for the lutes and voices.

The musical establishment, indeed, required

looking into. The Chapel Royal had been disbanded under the Protectorate and the first business was to see it restored to its former dignity. Charles recalled that a certain Captain Henry Cooke had taken part, with some distinction, on the royalist side during the late unhappy rebellion, and mindful of these services, he secured the Captain's appointment as Master of the Children. For the moment there were no children available, and for above a year after the re-opening of the Chapel 'the Orderers of the musick there were necessitated to supply the superior Parts of the music with cornets and men's feigned voices, there being not one Lad, for all that time, capable of singing his Part readily.' In the meantime, Captain Cooke was a man of proved energy and discipline, and he immediately set about scouring the country for likely lads, under the terms of the old Chapel Royal warrant which empowered him to impress choristers into the King's service. The Captain seems to have had a genius for discovering talent and nurturing it. Among his earliest set of boys were William Turner, Michael Wise, John Blow, all of whom were to become famous as composers, and little Pelham Humfrey, who soon became a favourite with the King.

Charles II's tastes were eminently secular, but his influence in changing the direction of English

music has probably been overrated.[1] True it is
that in the course of his travels abroad he had
acquired a love of the gayer type of music and
a passion for the violin. 'Pray get me pricked
down,' he writes from Bruges in 1655, 'as many
new Corrants and Sarrabands and other little
dances as you can, for I have got a small fidler
here that does not play ill on the fiddle.' If we
are to believe the reminiscent North, he disliked
any music to which he could not beat the time –
the vigilant eye of Pepys soon noticed that the
King was a little musical, for he beat time with his
hand during the anthem – and that along with his
love of dance-music Charles had 'an utter detes-
tation of fancies' (i.e. Fantasies for viols). When
Mr. Secretary Williamson invited him to hear a
consort of the old English music, Charles ridi-
culed him for his pains and remarked sarcastically
of the playing, 'Have I not ears, to judge as well as
anyone?' His Majesty, indeed, rather prided
himself on his ears. When the choir at the Chapel
Royal sang out of tune, he did not hesitate to
laugh outright. He himself sang a 'plump bass'
and would often try over a duet with the celebrated Mr. Gostling, Purcell's monumental bass

[1] 'The passion of this prince for French Music changed the
national taste' (Burney). Mr. H. Davey ('History of English
Music') follows suit: 'It was Charles II who killed the older
English School, vocal and instrumental alike, and who finally
killed the pride of the English in their music.'

singer, while the Duke of York accompanied on the guitar; or, with his hand on Tom D'Urfey's shoulder (an attitude he seems to have inherited from his father) he would hum over an Italian song, for which Tom had written some new words. He was, in fact, the first dilettante of his age. He had little or no literature, says a contemporary, but true and good sense and had got a right notion of style. To a passion for chemistry and navigation, he added an interest, if a slightly superficial one, in the arts. He discussed music with Evelyn and attended the rehearsals of Monsieur Grabu's opera at Whitehall, not failing to interject a few suggestions of his own. 'Peace be with the Ashes of so Good a King,' exclaims Dryden, in the preface to 'Albion and Albanius,' 'Let his Humane frailties be forgotten; and his Clemency and Moderation remembered with a grateful Veneration by Three Kingdoms. . . . For if writers be just to the memory of King Charles II they cannot deny him to have been an exact knower of Mankind and a perfect Distinguisher of their Talents.' But, in this matter, the poet Dryden was exercising his own particular talent for special pleading, as we shall see.

Charles was determined that the pleasures which he had enjoyed while on his travels should not be wanting now that he had come into his own again, but for the present nothing was to be gained by offending English susceptibilities. Most of the senior musicians who had survived the Interregnum were given posts either in the Church or as members of the King's Musick. King Louis' establishment was, of course, to be his model, but the names of the 'four-and-twenty fiddlers' are at the outset familiarly English, if we except that of the obscure Fitz. The aged Nicholas Laniere, whom we have already encountered as a Director of King Charles I's masques, came out of his retirement and was given the place of Master of the Musick. John Banister was sent over to France on special service to 'return with expedition,' no doubt after having made himself acquainted with the procedure of the twenty-four Violons du Roi. Baltzar, the Lubeck virtuoso, whose violin playing had astonished Anthony Wood a few years before at Oxford, was given a special place in the Private Musick, where his example could not fail to have a beneficent influence on the members of the King's band, but otherwise there were no immediate attempts to impose a foreign dominion. The Restoration was to apply to music no less than to matters of State.

Charles, who was, as Tudway remarks, a 'brisk and airy prince' was of a mind to have his band of violins[1] playing at the Royal Chapel on

---

[1] The band consisted of six treble, six counter-tenor, six tenor and six bass violins, the treble and counter-tenor instruments

the occasions on which he attended service, but it does not appear that he designed to create a revolution in church music, and the 'Symphonys and Ritornels' which he encouraged his composers to write in their anthems, much to the scandal of the graver sort, were rather a special token that he regarded his presence at church as a festive occasion, demanding a specially festive type of music. We have the specific statement of Tudway, who was a member of the choir at the Restoration and was later to compile a famous collection of church music, that Charles 'did not intend by this innovation to alter anything in the established way' or oblige the Cathedrals and churches throughout England to follow his example. Whether any man ever succeeded in penetrating His Majesty's real intentions is less certain, but there seems no reason in this case to doubt the word of a firsthand observer. At the same time, Charles had already fastened his eye on the promising talent which the industrious Captain Cooke had assembled about him, and 'in about four or five years time, some of the forwardest and brightest children of the Chappell, as Mr. Humphrey, Mr. Blow, Mr. Wise, etc., began to be Masters of a faculty in composing. This His Majesty greatly encouraged, by indulging their youthful fancys,

(according to Canon F. W. Galpin, 'Old English Instruments of Music') being identical, like our first and second violins.

so that every month at least and afterwards oftener they produced something new of this kind.'

For the time being, Charles seems to have set his hopes on the young English school, which was coming into existence under the admirable Captain Cooke, whose talent for instruction, if we are to judge by the success of his pupils, was equal to the sureness of instinct with which he alighted on promising material. A generation which had not known the old ways, Charles probably felt, was likely to prove more pliable than one which was prejudiced in favour of those solemn English traditions which he so much disliked. A few of the older musicians, who had received important posts, such as Christopher Gibbons at Westminster and Dr. Child at the Chapel Royal, made, it is true, some effort to 'comport themselves to the new-fangled ways,' but without much success. Circumstances were not a little against the church musicians in those early years of the restored monarchy. An extraordinary amount of their music had been burned during the Civil War; their organs had been destroyed, the choirs depleted and the style of singing had decayed. Old Thomas Mace, author of 'Musick's Monument,' that pious 'Remembrancer of the best Practical Musick, both Divine and Civil, that has ever been known to have been

39

in the World,' is still lamenting in 1676 that the Psalms of the Prophet David are (as he might say) 'tortur'd and tormented' by choirs which could scarcely rise above one man to a part. As for the music itself, it was not wholly irrecoverable, and three years after the Restoration there appeared a collection of Services and Anthems which gives some clue to the music that was available and indeed 'usually sung' in the Cathedrals and Churches throughout the country. The words alone were printed, but from these it is clear that a determined effort had been made to recover the tradition of English church music in the direct line of Tallis, Byrd and Gibbons.

The King's next move was to send young Pelham Humfrey, now seventeen and already a composer of anthems, over to France to gain some experience, at first hand, of the methods of the 'frenchifyed Italian,' Jean-Baptiste Lully, who had risen from the post of kitchen-scullion to be leader of the Petits Violons du Roi. Lully was at this period composing ballets, which were the rapture of the French court. His unscrupulous genius was soon to obtain complete ascendancy over the nascent French opera, on the final discomfiture of his rival Cambert, whom we shall meet later in London. He had already begun to develop the characteristic style of declamatory recitative, with its expressive inflexions and close adherence to the cadence and rhythm of the words, which he had evolved out of the methods of the Italians. He excelled equally in expressing moods of languid and melancholy emotion, of grief, pity, despair, and the 'tendres plaintes' of love, as in his lively feeling for natural effects, pastoral scenes, and the emanations of night, sleep, mystery and the like. He was feeling his way towards a descriptive instrumental style and developing a form of overture, consisting of a slow introduction with a plentiful use of dotted notes followed by a quick fugato section, which was to become standardised. Above all, he showed a great fondness for dance music, and he set his seal on the type of French opera, with its ballet and choruses used as an integral part of the dramatic action, which was to differentiate it from the Italian form with its greater reliance on the lyrical expressiveness of the voice.

It has been remarked as characteristic of Charles II's sardonic humour that he should have sent Pelham Humfrey to learn how to write English church music by studying under the most famous operatic composer of the day. It was part of the sweet revenge of time that Purcell, who certainly studied Humfrey's methods and was his pupil, should have learned later how to write English stage-music by following in Humfrey's footsteps in the matter of church composition.

Whether Humfrey was actually Lully's pupil we cannot say for certain, but in Paris at that time he could scarcely avoid coming under Lully's influence. He seems to have fallen very quickly into the French ways and returned to England, as Pepys remarks, an 'absolute monsieur.' But he did not confine his studies to France. The Secret Service accounts for the years 1664–66 contain, under their elastic disbursements, three entries relating to bounties paid to Humfrey to defray the expenses of his journey to France *and* Italy.

Charles seems to have endowed his favourite with a sort of travelling scholarship. In Italy the composer who would naturally attract Humfrey's attention was Carissimi, whose cantatas were extending to religious music the principles that had already been developed in the secular field of opera. It seems probable that Humfrey owed directly as much to the grace and charm of the Italian style as to the declamatory methods of Lully who had, of course, sipped at the Italian fountain himself. The element that Humfrey introduced into English church music was a delicately perfumed and slightly sentimental pathos. It is, on the other hand, absurd to say, as Burney does, that Humfrey was 'the first of our ecclesiastical composers who had the least idea of musical pathos in the expression of words

implying supplication or complaint.' Was there
no pathos in Byrd or Weelkes or Gibbons?

Humfrey was an enormously talented composer,
who died at the early age of twenty-seven, before
he had time to show whether he was going to be
an original genius or merely a very clever imitator of the dominant styles of the day. Like so
many of the Restoration composers he was pre-
cociously gifted and while still a boy had produced anthems which won the approval of the
critically minded Pepys. At the age of twenty he
was sharing the post of composer for the violins
with Matthew Locke, his senior by thirteen years,
and at twenty-five he succeeded Captain Cooke as
Master of the Chapel Royal children, although
Locke and others had better claims. With his
success and accomplishments, the personal fa-
vouritism of the King, whose verses he set to
music,[1] his man-of-the-world air which Pepys
called vanity, the way that he laughed at the
King's band (no doubt behind His Majesty's back)
and affected to despise everything English, he
must have been anything but a popular figure
among the group of older composers who were

[1] As, for instance:
　　I pass all my Hours in a Shady Old Grove,
　　But I live not the Day when I see not my Love,
　　I survey every walk now my Phyllis is Gone,
　　And sigh when I think we were there all alone.
　　Oh, then, 'tis oh then, that I think there's no Hell
　　　　　Like loving too well.

43

endeavouring to maintain their traditions in face of the changing times. Purcell, at the most, spent only a year under Humfrey at the Chapel Royal, but it was at an impressionable time – he was fourteen – and with his assimilative genius he could scarcely fail to be impressed by the novel procedures that Humfrey, with the royal connivance, was introducing into English music.

Apart from his use of the declamatory recitative style, charm rather than depth would seem to be the characteristic feature of Humfrey's church music. He writes much in the minor mode, and for the expression of pathos employs those diminished or augmented intervals which he perhaps derived from the example of Lully, though indeed he might have sought them out among the works of the older English school. Like many consciously modern composers he preferred to build his house with new bricks rather than quarry for antique stone. And, like them, he sometimes gives the impression of using his materials because they happen to be fashioned to his hand, rather than because they are especially appropriate. When he 'sings to the Lord a new song' he is apt to be content to do so by means of a new chord or a new inflexion. The rather prim little anthem 'Rejoice in the Lord' shows him at his most graceful; the use of a refrain, the alternations of triple and quadruple

measures, the general cleanness of style, all is
charming, if not very profound. But Humfrey is
an important figure, if only because he typifies
the new spirit which was creeping into English
church music.

We may leave him for the moment pursuing his
studies abroad and turn to glance at the general
condition of English music in the first decade of
Charles II's reign. The French manner of instrumental music, Roger North tells us, 'did not
gather so fast as to make a revolution all at once;
but during the greater part of Charles II's reign,
the old music was used in the country and in
many meetings and societies in London. But the
treble viol was disregarded and the violin took its
place.' The change was neither so abrupt nor so
sudden as has often been implied. The amateurs,
indeed, clung to the older instruments. At Oxford, which had been during the Commonwealth
one of the strongholds of musical practice, the
violin, as Anthony Wood tells us, was esteemed to
be an instrument 'only belonging to a common
fiddler,'[1] and though Christopher Simpson, in his
'Division Violist,' published on the eve of the
Restoration, follows the usual English custom of

[1] In Thomas Southerne's comedy 'The Maid's Last Prayer'
(1693) it is still apparently possible for a character to be insulted
by being called a 'fidler.'
    'Why, did he call me a fidler?'
    'He said you were a wretched scraper, only
fit to play to a garland upon a May-Day.'

inveighing against novelties and asserts that the
music of the viols is 'now much neglected,' it
hardly escapes notice that his treatise was re-
issued a few years later and even reached a third
edition in 1712 – facts which are open to the pre-
sumption that the instruments were still being
studied. Old Mace, publishing his magnum opus
in 1676, utters a tirade against the new fashions
with special reference to the ' scoulding violins,'
but his account of the 'Noble Lute' and 'Generous
Viol' was presumably not of mere antiquarian
interest. And with all Charles II's preference for
the violin, his establishment included posts for
both these instruments. Charles Colman, who
was appointed 'Musician in Ordinary for the
violls' after the Restoration, received a similar appointment in the next reign and even towards the
end of the century foreign instrumentalists were
coming to England to study the bass-viol. 'You
need not' says Simpson, characteristically, 'seek
Outlandish Authors, especially for Instrumental
Musick; no Nation (in my opinion) being equal
to the English in that way.'

But while the more seriously inclined amateurs
and professional musicians were clinging dog-
gedly to the traditional music, it was clear that the
wind of change was beginning to blow from
another direction. It has often been said that the
Restoration brought about the triumph of the

modern, secular spirit in English musical art. So far as music needed secularising (and manifestly there had always been a secular development lying outside the ecclesiastical tradition) the decisive steps had already been taken under the Puritan régime, which for the time being closed the avenues of religious music. Hitherto the professional musician had perforce to rely on church appointments and the patronage of the nobility. Thrown upon his own resources, he now begins to emerge as a public teacher and performer. The arrival of the virtuoso performer signalised the most decisive change in the musical outlook of the period. Roger North, from the vantage of the early eighteenth century, sums up this change of outlook with his usual shrewdness, when he says, 'The flourishing of an art or science, is the number and value of the professors and those obtaining their end, which in music is pleasure, and an innocuous Imploy of spare time, with a recreation. In the intervalls of business, the gain and credit is egregious; all which fell out when the Art was plain and practicable and most sober familys in England affected it. Now it is come to pass, that ffew but professors can handle it, and the value is derived upon high flights and numbers of capitall performers, which may have brought an audience but the promiscuous and diffused practise of musick in remote parts about England is utterly confounded. And an ostentatious pride hath taken Apollo's chair and almost subverted his monarchy.'

There was throughout the 17th century a growing consciousness on the part of professional musicians of their status as members of a close fraternity. ✓Charles I had granted a charter to the musicians of the City of Westminster, but it had lain dormant throughout the troubled period of the Civil Wars. Nicholas Laniere became the first Marshal of the Corporation of Music in 1636, and it was he who was apparently the moving spirit in its renascence in 1661, immediately after the Restoration, when he again appears as Marshal. The Corporation was empowered to make orders regulating the practice and profession of music. (It is amusing to note that Matthew Locke and Christopher Gibbons were mulcted of £10 in the year 1663 for certain transgressions of the Corporation's rules.) The orders of the Corporation include the licensing of teachers, as well as the regulation of the activities of the 'waites' and 'common minstrells.' On 20th January 1662 it is ordered that 'Edward Sadler, for his insufficiency in the art of musique, be from henceforward silenced and disabled from the exercise of any kinds in publique houses or meetings' and on 16th July 1664 there is a warrant for 'the apprehension of all persons professing the art and science of musick, playing at any play-houses, game-houses, taverns, victualling-houses or any place in the city of London and Westminster, without the approbation and lycense of the Marshall and Corporation of musique.' Again on 28th June 1669, we meet with a name, which is to figure importantly in Henry Purcell's career, that of Josiah Priest, who with certain others is apprehended 'for teaching, practising and executing music in companies or otherwise, without the approbation or lycense of the Marshall and Corporation of musick, in contempt of his Majesty's authority and the power granted to the Marshall and Corporation.'

It is not difficult to see in these measures an attempt on the part of the professional musicians to protect their interests against the competition of the inexpert, which with the growth of music publishing and the appearance of popular text-books was threatening their livelihood, as also perhaps an effort to stem the tide of foreign artists, who began to arrive in numbers in the country during the early years of Charles II's reign. One of Charles' first acts had been to grant a licence to the Italian Gentileschi for the establishment of an opera-house in London, the members of the company to be designated His Majesty's Servants. We hear nothing more of this project, and during the next few years various schemes were propounded for introducing opera on the Italian model with 'scenes and machines,' only to prove equally abortive. His Majesty's ambitions, no doubt, exceeded the limitations of his exchequer. Indeed, his treatment of his own musicians in this matter was shortly to become notorious. Salaries were allowed to fall into arrears and there was a continual series of petitions from members of the Royal Musick for the payment of monies long overdue. The flattering title of His Majesty's Servants was clearly not sufficient to induce the foreigners to embark on the doubtful undertaking of presenting opera in England, in default of something more substantial than the promise of royal favour. At the same time Charles did his best to gratify his passion for foreign entertainments by encouraging French and Italian musicians to settle in London, and in 1666 he took the decisive step of appointing Monsieur Grabu Master of the English Chamber Musick.

Louis Grabu seems to have arrived in this country shortly after the Restoration, and to have been given a place as violinist in the King's Private Musick. His fortunes rose rapidly and he was very soon in possession of a large income and the most desirable positions at Court. Charles seems at first to have showered favours and money on Grabu, and it was probably on account of these and similar extravagances that he found himself faced in 1669 with a demand for retrenchment in his private expenditure. Charles, however, remained firm, and with the example of the French court ever in his mind, refused to hear of any interference with 'our foure and twenty violins together with the master of our musick.' He had already promoted Monsieur Grabu to a position of authority over John Banister as leader of the band of violins – Banister having, it is said, thoughtlessly remarked that he considered English violinists better than the French.[1] The post was a lucrative one and there seems in Banister's case to have been a little scandal about his administration of the monies due to the band, to account for his dismissal. However that may be, the change was made and Monsieur Grabu acquired the prestige and the emoluments that Banister lost. The situation was not calculated to pacify the English court musicians, already irritated by the chronic delays in the payment of their salaries. And it is a little ironical to reflect that under Grabu were people like the great Jenkins (though no longer very active) the impetuous Locke and William Young, who had won fame abroad and

---

[1] There seems to have been some justification for Banister's remark. Lully found that not one half the French musicians, who formed the Petits Violons du Roi, could read at sight. When Corelli's sonatas arrived in Paris, there were not three persons who could be found to play them.

had written violin sonatas far in advance of their time.[1]

✓ It is usually held that Grabu was a mediocrity whose chief recommendation for Charles was that he was French. Contemporary opinion seems to have been equally severe, perhaps for the same reason. Pepys, who calls him 'Mons. Grebus,' went to hear a concert of his works at Whitehall and declared that the 'manner of setting of words and repeating them out of order' made him 'sick.' Not to mend matters, Pelham Humfrey, fresh from his experiences abroad and full of his own conceit, gave out that Monsieur Grabu was no better than a charlatan – 'he understands nothing, nor can play on any instrument and so cannot compose' – and that he would soon 'give him a lift out of his place.' Pepys, however, allows that Grabu had brought the band to play 'very just.'

✓ For the present, the sun continued to shine on the Frenchman. In 1673 there arrived in London Robert Cambert, whose pupil Grabu had been. Cambert was one of the founders of the French opera and had taken part in the formation of the 'Académie de Musique' which was simply an institution for the production of opera, a theatrical venture. Outwitted and outman-œuvred by the more astute Lully in the favours of

[1] If indeed the William Young mentioned in the records is to be identified with the famous composer.

the French King, Cambert had been forced, by ill-success and debts, to take refuge in England. He immediately began to make plans for an English Academy of Music, after the French model, and in this he sought the collaboration of Grabu. The upshot of this alliance was the production, early in the following year, of Cambert's opera 'Ariane, ou le mariage de Bacchus,' performed in honour of the wedding of Mary of Modena to James, Duke of York, and brought up-to-date and adapted by Grabu.[1] It seems probable that French singers were brought over for the performance and in that case there can be little doubt of the language in which it was sung. The music was originally Cambert's, but Grabu touched up the libretto and wrote additional numbers; a fulsome prologue in praise of Charles and England was added, and several scenes and characters inserted. The libretto alone has survived and is prefaced by a servile dedication in which Charles is hailed as the patron saint of the new Academy, and this 'fortunate isle' declared to be a haven of refuge for (in other words) ship-wrecked Frenchmen.

The exact causes of Grabu's sudden fall from grace, after these auspicious openings, are lost in obscurity. There was possibly some misdemeanour

[1] M. Romain Rolland is apparently alone in thinking that Grabu 'wrote the music for the translation of Cambert's "Ariane," or at least adapted it to English words.'

in connection with the loan of certain scenery of which he had been granted the use from the King's playhouse in Whitehall, for the production of the French opera at the theatre in Bridge's Street. Grabu having failed to return the scenery within the specified period, a warrant was issued a month later for its delivery into the hands of Sir Christopher Wren, at that time in charge of the *décor* at Whitehall. Whatever the reason may have been, the records of the year 1674 show that Monsieur Grabu had vacated his place, while remaining a creditor for sundry arrears of salary, and that Nicholas Staggins ruled in his stead as Master of the Private Musick. It was Staggins who wrote the music for Crowne's Masque 'Calisto' later in the same year and in whose person the author professed to trace 'the hopes of seeing in a very short time a master of music in England equal to any France or Italy have produced.' Purcell was in his sixteenth year. Mr. Staggins, though he became a doctor of music and a university professor, lived to falsify the pious expectations that were formed of him.

But Charles' appetite for French Kickshaws[1] was not sated. Already, in 1671, he had persuaded Betterton, the actor, to visit Paris for the

[1] A common Restoration expression for trivial and superficial innovations.

purpose of studying French operatic production. Betterton had seen the performance, on a superb scale, of Lully's *tragédie-ballet* 'Psyche' and on his return got Shadwell to make an English adaptation for the new theatre in Dorset Gardens. 'Psyche,' which Locke somewhat romantically called 'The English Opera,' was produced in 1675 with music by Locke and Draghi, an Italian who had settled in London and was later to figure in the famous contest with Purcell and Blow for the erection of the Temple organ. There was a ballet by the French choreographist, St. Andrée, and no doubt some of those artists concerning whom Downes, the prompter, wrote that 'Mr. Betterton to gratify the desires and Fancies of the Nobility and Gentry procured from abroad the best Dancers and Singers . . . who being Exorbitantly Expensive produced small Profit to him and his company but vast Gain to themselves.' Two years later there was another French opera at Whitehall and Charles, finding his tastes more expensive than his purse would allow, threw open his private theatre to the public and had money taken at the doors. In 1683 Betterton was again in Paris and failing in his efforts to secure a French opera company, happened upon the unfortunate Monsieur Grabu, now in very reduced circumstances and still a creditor to his English majesty. The meeting resulted in Grabu's return and, an event of much significance, his introduction to the English poet-laureate, John Dryden. Purcell was now twenty-four.

Dryden's attitude to English music and to the new forms of stage-entertainment which were presently to make things so difficult for heroic dramatists, was curiously vacillating. He lived at a time when writers for the stage, while professing an unbounded admiration for the works of Shakespeare, did not scruple to subject those works to the most tasteless revision, under the impression that they needed clarifying and bringing up-to-date. Had these things been done in the name of opera it would have been well enough, for opera has always made such depredations and has largely subsisted on garbled versions of famous plays. But they were done, apparently, in the name of commonsense, though the result was frequently common nonsense. Dryden was not the least industrious, though assuredly the most skilful, of the adapters, and an original genius, to boot. He was a professional man of letters, the first completely professional English man of letters. He had already, in conjunction with Davenant, brought out a version of the 'Tempest' which held the stage for many years and was later, in a further adaptation, to receive the support of Purcell's music. Dryden, as a literary man with, if we are to judge, very little

56

real taste for music, could not view the advent
of spectacular musical productions without mis-
giving. It is thus that we find him delivering a
significant Prologue at the opening of the new
King's Theatre in 1674:

> 'Twere folly now a stately pile to raise
> To build a playhouse while you throw down plays,
> Whilst scenes, machines and empty Operas reign
> And for the Pencil you the Pen disdain.
> While Troops of famished Frenchmen hither drive,
> And laugh at those upon whose Alms they live.
> Our English Authors vanish and give place
> To these new Conquerors of the Norman race.

But Dryden, it has been observed, was always
ready to respect a *fait accompli*, and having con-
secrated his 'Heroick Stanzas' to the memory
of his Highness Oliver and written a poem on the
happy return of His Sacred Majesty Charles II,
he was not the man to be totally unaccommoda-
ting in the matter of 'scenes, machines and empty
operas,' however much and sincerely he might
fulminate in the meantime. As for the 'famished
Frenchmen' and 'Italian merry-andrews,' apparently these were the sort of people that were
responsible for such degrading productions, and
no one had yet remarked that it was unnecessary
to live.

It was accordingly for Monsieur Grabu, once
more basking in the sun of royal favour, that Dryden wrote his grand patriotic spectacle 'Albion

and Albanius,' designed to be the prologue to a yet greater spectacle 'King Arthur,' in which the glories of our blood and state were to be celebrated. Originally there was no Albanius; there was simply Albion – Charles himself, whose meritorious reign was to be the subject of this splendid allegorical fiction. But as the rehearsals were nearing their end an unfortunate event occurred. Charles died. It therefore became necessary to extend the scope of the work so as to include his successor, James, who figures as Albanius. . . . Monsieur Grabu's trials, however, were not yet over.

Dryden, duly embarked on his operatic career, took occasion in the preface to deliver himself of some theories concerning the nature of opera (as that it must contain Gods and heroic figures and, being beyond human nature, must admit of 'marvellous and surprizing conduct,' as indeed it usually does) and incidentally he pays a handsome tribute to his collaborator. 'The best judges and those too of the best quality, who have honoured his rehearsals with their presence,[1] have no less commended the happiness of his genius and skill. These and other qualities have raised M. Grabu to a degree above any man who shall pretend to be his rival on our stage. And let me have the liberty to add one thing, that he has so exactly

[1] The reference is to Charles.

expressed my sense in all places where I intended to move the passions, that he seems to have entered into my thoughts and to have been the poet as well as the composer. This I say, not to flatter him, but to do him right; because among some English musicians and their scholars who are sure to judge after them, the imputation of being a Frenchman is enough to make a party, who maliciously endeavour to decry him.' But, he patriotically adds, 'When any of our countrymen excel him I shall be glad, for the sake of Old England, to be shown my error.' Purcell was twenty-six, but it took Dryden another five years before he realised his error.

Monsieur Grabu is even more outspoken on the merits of the music, his music. 'As the subject of this opera,' he remarks, 'is naturally magnificent, it could not but excite my genius, and raise it to a greater height in the composition – even so as to surpass itself.' His only fear is that the English singers are not sufficiently excellent to do him full justice. It is, indeed, exceedingly probable that Grabu surpassed himself. The opera was the most spectacular that had yet been seen on the English stage and the merits of Dryden's text, granted its purpose, were considerable. Grabu's genius, such as it was, could scarcely fail to have been excited by the prospect of the clouds dividing and Juno appearing 'in a Machine Drawn by Peacocks;

59

while a Symphony is playing, it moves gently forward and as it descends, it opens and Discovers the Tail of the Peacock, which is so large that it almost fills the opening of the Stage between Scene and Scene.'[1] That the score was not completely negligible may be gathered from the fact that Purcell seems to have studied it with some attention. Grabu's use of instruments had, in fact, a certain point. Where he was most at sea was in his treatment of the words, which is scarcely wonderful seeing that he was working in a foreign tongue. North's comment that 'Albion' was 'in English but of a french Genius' sums up the whole matter. Compared with Purcell, Grabu was, indeed, a mere mediocrity. French writers have taken a more tolerant view of his work and are perhaps right in suggesting that 'Albion' helped to awaken the emulation of his more distinguished successor. Purcell was not above taking a leaf out of the book of a rival in whom he could hardly avoid discerning a talent immeasurably inferior to his own as a musician. And when a few years later he published his music to 'Dioclesian' in a form similar to that of Grabu's opera, it was as though he were throwing out a direct challenge to public judgment. Dryden veered round with the best possible grace. In Mr. Purcell, he said, they had

[1] The scene of Juno and the Peacocks seems to have been a popular effect with the Restoration producers. It recurs in Purcell's 'Fairy Queen.'

60

at length found an Englishman equal to the best abroad. And this time, as it turned out, the swan was not a goose.

Monsieur Grabu's misfortunes did not end with the production of 'Albion and Albanius.' The opera had been running for a few nights only when another catastrophe occurred. The Duke of Monmouth landed in the West and the country was immediately thrown into a turmoil. 'Albion' was withdrawn, at the moment it was promising to be a success, after six performances, 'which not Answering half the charge they were at, Involv'd the company very much in Debt.'[1] Grabu's reward was a spate of satirical verses:

> Each actor on the stage his luck bewailing,
> Finds that his loss is infallibly true;
> Smith, Nokes and Leigh in a feverish railing,
> Curse Poet and Painter, and Monsieur Grabu.

His only consolation appears to have been that James II paid up the arrears of salary which were due to him from his late Majesty. But the clouds closed in again, and when they divided, there was a brighter star in the firmament.

[1] Downes.

Chapter III

PURCELL AND HIS AGE

IF, as an ironical writer has been pleased to allege, ignorance is the first requisite of the historian, then the biographers of Purcell must be accounted singularly well equipped. But the ignorance which consists in ignoring, in shutting a careful eye to the superfluity of detail, is rather a different matter from the sheer scantiness of authenticated fact which we meet with in the case of a Shakespeare or a Purcell. There is, in the biographical sense, no real life of Purcell. He left no letters, a will that tells us, as wills are apt to do, that he died in the full possession of his faculties, some formal and not very illuminating dedications and prefaces to his few published works; and he died, the most famous English musician of his age, universally admired, and was buried, with great ceremony, in Westminster Abbey.[1] That anyone so celebrated and respected in his own day should have left so few memorials,

[1] 'Dr. Purcell was interred at Westminster in a magnificent manner. He is much lamented as a very great master of music.' ('Post Boy,' Nov. 28, 1695.) But this posthumous Doctorate has not been confirmed.

outside his compositions, is indeed a little disheartening to conscientious biographers. The very date of his birth is unknown.[1] His life is largely a matter of conjecture, hidden away in the brief obscurities of official records, a tale of official appointments and professional activities, with only some incidental clues that he was a human being at all.

Roger North, James II's Attorney-General, who certainly came into personal contact with him, is content with a short reference to 'Mr. H. Purcell, the Orpheus Britannicus, who unhappily began to show his Great skill before the reforme of musick *al Italliana*, and while he was warm in the pursuit of it, Dyed, but a greater musical genius England never had.' – a statement which is, at least, ambiguous. The inquisitive Pepys, who could surely have given us some scraps from the current gossip, thoughtlessly closed his diary when Purcell was a child of ten. We search in vain through the memoirs and journals of the time for anything more than extravagant adulation and expressions of admiring astonishment. Dr. Blow could think of no better memorial to himself than to claim to be the master of the famous Mr. Henry Purcell, but few people claimed the virtue of being Purcell's pupils. Contemporaries and successors alike seem to have been entirely and uncritically

[1] Probably some time between June and August 1659.

overawed by his powers. He had a few minor imitators, such as his brother Daniel, and one great and overmastering follower, George Frederic Handel. For the rest, such was his prestige that Croft, in his setting of the Burial Service, could retire abashed before a verse set by his famous predecessor and incorporate it bodily in his composition. That he had 'a most commendable ambition of exceeding every one of his time and succeeded in it without contradiction,'[1] seems as clear to us to-day as it did to his contemporaries. It was not till the time of Arne that there was any breath of criticism and Arne's criticism was less just than ill-natured. Overwhelmed with praise from that day to this, Purcell has since paid the penalty of the English talent for extolling what it most neglects.

He steps out of the pages of the Lord Chamberlain's records as a 'late child of his Majesty's Chappell Royal, whose voice is changed and gon from the Chappell,' complete with a yearly allowance, a quantity of fine linen and a felt hat. The voice changed to that of a high counter-tenor or male alto which was later to delight audiences at the Cecilian celebrations with its 'incredible graces.' At the Chapel Royal he had as masters Captain Cooke, whose theatrical propensities and Italianate style of singing must have impressed him at

[1] Tudway.

64

an early age, and Pelham Humfrey, who during his last year was introducing the new French-Italian style in his anthems. Blow did not come in as master of the Chapel Royal children till 1674, a year after Purcell had left, but he had already been appointed organist at Westminster Abbey at the precocious age of twenty,[1] and it was here that Purcell came under his influence when, a boy of seventeen, he was appointed copyist.

Blow was twenty-eight. His relation to Purcell bears some resemblance to that of Haydn to Mozart. Born ten or eleven years before him, he survived Purcell by thirteen years. His character is a little mysterious, and we do not know whether his faculty for resigning important posts to his brilliant pupils (Purcell at Westminster and Mr. Jerry Clarke at St. Paul's) was due to expediency or generosity. Purcell hailed him as 'one of the greatest Masters in the world.' That he had a sharp tongue we know from the incident of the Jesuit priest Petre, who, reporting James II's commendation of one of Blow's anthems, ventured to add his own comment that it was too long. 'That,' said Blow, 'is the opinion of one fool and

[1] But this prococity on the part of English musicians was not new. Byrd became organist of Lincoln Cathedral at twenty and Bull was organist at Hereford at the same age. It is possible, however, that the post of organist was not formerly held in so high esteem as it is to-day. Purcell is, indeed, referred to in a memorandum of the Westminster Abbey Chapter minutes as 'Mr. Purcell, the organ-blower.'

I heed it not.' His eminence as a teacher may be judged by the success of his pupils. We meet him in the Cheque Book records fetching choir-boys from various parts of the country for service in the King's Chapel, and in the number and variety of his posts, as in the scope of his public activities, he is excelled only by Purcell. Dr. Burney, that eminent maligner of English musicians of this period, devotes several pages to an exposure of his 'crudities,' matters which nowadays evoke more admiration than displeasure. 'It does not appear,' says the Doctor, viciously, 'that Purcell, whom he did himself the honour to call his scholar, or Crofts or Clarke, his pupils, ever threw notes about at Random, in his manner, or insulted the ear with lawless discords which no concords can render tolerable.' Blow's lawlessness is, however, not so wanton as it seemed to Dr. Burney. He remains, at some points, a more ruggedly unconventional composer than Purcell and his harmonic experiments and adventurous modulations are apt to startle the ear in a way that Purcell, with all his gift for surprising turns, rarely does. But in other respects he was an admirable corrective to the facile Humfrey. In him one feels a much greater kinship with the spirit of the older church composers, a more solid musicianship, coupled with a purely personal outlook on the new resources of the time. And the apprenticeship which Purcell served under him at Westminster was much more important than his year under Humfrey at the Chapel Royal.

Apart from his direct contact with Blow, the post of copyist at the Abbey would bring Purcell into touch with a vast amount of music of a traditional character. We do not know what was the music Purcell actually copied during these years. Westminster Abbey had been one of the chief sufferers from the Puritan excesses. The organ had been destroyed and the pipes bartered for pots of ale by the intoxicated Puritan forces. Blow's immediate predecessors had been two musicians of the older school, Bryan and Christopher Gibbons, who held the post of organist for short terms after the Restoration, Gibbons having also been the music copyist. From the catalogue of services and anthems transcribed into the Chapel Royal books at this period we observe, along with a certain amount of music by Byrd, Farrant and Whyte of the earlier period, an increasing amount of work by the newer composers such as Humfrey, Wise and Blow. But it is fair to assume that the music at the Abbey was on more conservative lines. For one thing the band of violins did not play there except on state occasions, and therefore the style of the music would be more definitely choral – much of it, indeed, may have been unaccompanied. We cannot explain the music which Purcell was later to write for the church and theatre except on the assumption that he had a thorough grounding in polyphonic technique, and where was he more likely to have gained his technique than during the years of his apprenticeship as copyist at the Abbey ? Four years later, in 1680, Blow relinquished his post as organist in favour of his brilliant pupil. The curious fact is that a few years after becoming the Abbey organist, Purcell resumed the post of copyist. Was it a mere matter of adding to his income or did he feel that he had still something to learn from the older composers ? We know that, like Bach, he was an assiduous transcriber of other men's works, and that he copied, among other things, anthems by Tomkins, that greatly neglected composer, who was the last of the great line of Byrd and Gibbons.[1]

The Chapel Royal system was admirably calculated to produce a continuity of musical training. Purcell in later years was to lament 'the unhappiness of his Education' which had omitted to

[1] Thomas Tomkins (d. 1656) was a pupil of Byrd. He is said to have left over a hundred anthems, including one in twelve real parts. Purcell copied the anthems of several composers into a MS. book now in the Fitzwilliam Museum, Cambridge, and later used it for his own fair copy album. It is on a fly-leaf of this book that he has written at the beginning of one of his own works the words, 'God bless Mr. Henry Purcell 1682, September ye 10th.'

include the Italian language (that fashionable acquisition) but few musicians can have had less cause to reflect upon the incompleteness of their technical training for the art of music. The children of the Chapel Royal were no doubt given a general education, some even proceeding to the University, but their training in most cases was clearly vocational. They were, in short, articled to members of the musical profession, who kept them, clothed them and tended them in sickness, upon an allowance from the King's Exchequer. Purcell, losing his father in his sixth year, was brought up by his uncle, Thomas, who refers to him affectionately as 'my son.' Both the elder Purcells were Gentlemen of the Chapel Royal and Thomas held several important appointments at Court, where he appears in association with Humfrey as composer and master of the band of violins. With such antecedents there was little doubt as to the direction of the son's career.

Purcell's first appointment was that of Assistant to John Hingston as Keeper and repairer of the King's wind instruments. It was an important post and, when on Hingston's death he succeeded to full authority, it became a not unprofitable one. At any rate, Purcell kept it to the end of his career. Musical appointments at the time were not as a whole remarkably lucrative and were rendered less so by the incorrigible procrastinations of the

Royal Exchequer. Salaries often went by default for years at a time, and it became necessary for musicians to secure their livelihood by holding several positions at once – the custom has survived. Purcell was a magnificent pluralist, in this matter, as in others, outstripping all the composers of his time. The tale of his appointments is a remarkable one. To the technical posts already mentioned he added those of Composer for the violin in succession to Locke (1677, aet. 18) organist of Westminster Abbey (1680), organist at the Chapel Royal (1682), Composer in ordinary to the King's Musick (1683) and 'harpsicall-player' to King James II. In addition he seems at one time to have held the post of organist at St. Margaret's, Westminster, and during the latter years of his life to have been attached as a regular composer to the theatre in Dorset Gardens. He had a number of desirable pupils among the aristocracy, was connected with Mr. Josiah Priest's academy for young gentlewomen, for which he wrote 'Dido and Aeneas,' and was in regular demand as a composer of occasional pieces at the music meetings, feasts and festivals of the time. From the start all paths seem to have been open to him. He shared with Blow the task of writing those Birthday Odes and Welcome Songs, which flattered the royal ears with praises that sound to us somewhat grotesque. He wrote Odes

for St. Cecilia's Day from the date of its first
public observance, pieces for special gatherings
such as the 'Yorkshire Feast' in London, Coronation Anthems, Funeral Anthems, and even an
anthem for the felicitous prospect of an addition
to the royal family. He wrote for the theatre, the
church and the home, with equal success. There
is nothing to show that his public life was overcast
by a single shadow, apart from a trivial dispute
with the Dean and Chapter of Westminster which
nearly cost him his post; while of his private
sorrows it may be said that we know nothing
beyond the fact that three of his children died
in infancy – there was probably consumption
in the family. Purcell himself died early in
his thirty-seventh year, possibly from the same
cause.

It is a record from which we can deduce no
picture, except that of an enormously successful
and ceaselessly active professional musician, a
record which is barely supplemented by the few
occasions on which he speaks in the first (or prefer-
ably, the third) person in his published works.
Endowed by his contemporaries (or such of them
as have left their unanimous testimony) with
incredible perfections both as an artist and a
man, and by posterity with an unbelievable
precociousness (from which he has only been
tardily rescued by a critical examination of the

dates of his works)[1] he passes across the stage of
history, a slightly unreal figure, scarcely human,
and something less than divine. This Purcell,
who wrote catches which even the cold eye of
historical scholarship cannot contemplate without
blinking (and which must therefore, in the Purcell
Society's edition, be communicated in decorous
paraphrases which Purcell never knew); this
organist of Westminster Abbey who wrote music
for the farces, heroic bombasts and spectacular
pantomimes of the less than decorous Restoration
stage, and who would as soon make a song to be
sung about the streets as write an anthem for a
cathedral service; this Court composer who could
be cheerful to order even when confronted with
the most dismal doggerel that ever pretended to be
poetry; who could write one perfect opera and
never attempt another – remains a little remote
and inexplicable. For one thing we have to be
thankful. History has been unsuccessful in
attaching to him any of those picturesque fictions
and mythical attributes, with which the repu-
tations of so many great composers have had to
contend. Apart from the fact that he now seems
to us to have been no more precocious (except

[1] In this, as in so many matters, the late W. Barclay Squire
has placed all students of Purcell under a lasting obligation.
'Dido & Aeneas' has at various times been referred to Purcell's
22nd, 19th and even his 17th year. Mr. Squire, by his brilliant
deductions, placed it as late as the 30th year of the composer's
life.

in his greater mastery) than many young composers of his time, the only partially successful fiction that has been fastened on him is a discreditable one: that he died from a cold after being locked out by his wife. But Sir John Hawkins' credentials are more than a little suspect.[1]

His path is everywhere haunted by the unrevealing adjective 'famous.' It seems impossible for any of the writers of his own or the succeeding age to mention him except in terms of that fame of his, which has become so obscure. He is the 'famous Mr. Henry Purcell' and that is all that need, apparently, be said.[2] This contagion of his fame has spread to subsequent writers who must perforce raise to the pitch of celebrity those few incidents (such as the Temple organ contest and the dispute with the Dean and Chapter) in order

[1] Internal evidence, such as the catch 'Jack thou'rt a toper,' which contains references to the domestic strife likely to be caused by 'coming late' and another 'My wife has a tongue' cannot probably be taken with much seriousness. Purcell certainly composed an extraordinary number of convivial catches and in the collections of the 'Catch Club' he is represented by some of the more bawdy examples. Dr. Aldrich wrote a smoking catch in which rests were provided for the singers to take a puff at their pipes. Purcell enlarged upon this by writing a drunken catch in which rests were provided for eructations. His sense of humour in these works seems to have been frankly Rabelaisian.

[2] 'A music book intituled Harmonia Sacra will shortly be printed for Mr. Playford. I need not say anything more to recommend it to you than that you will find in it many of Mr. Henry Purcell's admirable Composures. As they charm all men, they are universally extoll'd, and even those who know him no otherwise than by his Notes, are fond of expressing their Sense of his Merit.' ('Gentleman's Journal,' June 1694.)

that they may disguise the void that obtains all round. But these public events actually tell us very little of the man. We see him a little less dimly as the friend of the Rev. John Gostling 'that stupendous base' for whom he wrote so many heroic solos in his anthems and to whom he sent a satirical catch on the viol, an instrument which Gostling favoured; or in association with John Shore, one of a remarkable family of trumpet-players, for whom he wrote his dazzling trumpet passages; or again, if the story may be trusted, giving 'Young' Bowen, the singer, his head in the matter of gracing a passage in his music – always in love with brilliant device and virtuoso execution.[1] To such a man the chance of introducing Father Smith's new organ at the Temple would be chiefly valuable for the opportunity it gave him of experimenting with the additional 'quarter-tones' and the increased range of keys which Smith's instrument made feasible.

We meet him for the first time in person in the set of sonatas for two violins which he published in 1683. He had recently been appointed one of his Majesty's composers in ordinary, and these sonatas,

---

[1] Purcell taught John Shore's sister (afterwards Mrs. Colley Cibber) to sing and play the harpsichord, besides writing several songs for her. The incident of Jemmy Bowen is told in Anthony Aston's supplement to Cibber's 'Lives.' 'He when practising a song set by Mr. Purcell, some of the Music told him to grace and run a division in such a place. O let him alone, said Mr. Purcell, he will grace it more naturally than you or I can teach him.'

he professes, in a somewhat overcharged dedication to the Sacred Charles, are the 'immediate
results' of the royal favour. But in the preface he
speaks his mind more clearly. He does not waste
time on 'learned Encomions' as to the beauty and
charms of music, in accordance with the usual
practice. He will go straight to the point. 'For
its author, he has faithfully endeavour'd a just
imitation of the most fam'd Italian masters;
principally to bring the Seriousness and gravity
of that sort of musick into vogue, and reputation
among our Country-men, whose humour, 'tis
time now, should begin to loathe the levity and
balladry of our neighbours' (sc. the French).
This, coupled with the dedication to his Franco-
phile majesty, was scarcely tactful, but the reference to the Italians probably served to alleviate
the sting of the offending passage. Exactly who
those 'fam'd Italian masters' were that are cited
as models is not so clear. There were few Italian
sonatas available at the time, unless it were in
manuscript. Vitali had published a set of sonatas
at Bologna in 1677, but he had been preceded as
early as 1653 by William Young, an Englishman
in the service of the Archduke Ferdinand Charles,
who had issued a set of sonatas at Innsbrück in
that year, to which the resemblances are even
more curious. The fact that Purcell might have
'faithfully endeavoured a just imitation' of the best

English masters, is carefully concealed. Unfortunately we can only take Purcell's word for it, even if we take it with a grain of salt.[1]

Charles was by no means exclusively wedded to the French school. His favourite composer is said to have been Carissimi – at least, he incited Blow to make a composition in imitation of the Italian master – and it is possible that towards the end of his reign the fashions had begun to swing over to the direction of the Italian music. North, indeed, assigns the change from French to Italian taste to the coming of Nicola Matteis, who turned up in England shortly after the Restoration and astonished the cognoscenti with his 'noveltys and high flights' on the violin ('every stroke,' says the erudite North, 'was a mouthfull'), besides being a virtuoso on the guitar, in the mysteries of which he instructed James II. 'It rests onely to Intimate that this forreigners teaching and promiscuous joyning with the English in consort musick and conversation, Bredd such a favour for the Itallian manner that most musicall gentlemen openly professed to owne that and no other manner.' But the fact remains that Matteis published nothing till after the appearance of Purcell's sonatas,

[1] It has been suggested that Purcell's eldest son, John Baptist, was named after Vitali. But these were the Christian names of at least three other well-known contemporaries – Lully, Bassani and Draghi. It is much more likely to have been a compliment to Draghi.

though his example may well have afforded an impulse to the young English composer's interest in the violin. The only Italian master who could have challenged comparison with him was Corelli, and by a curious coincidence Corelli's first set of sonatas were published in the same year, but Purcell could not have seen them at the time he wrote his own set, unless Matteis or some of those adventurous young men 'of the best quality and estate' who were passing to and fro between England and Italy about this time, brought them over in manuscript. Matteis, however, was a virtuoso and played only his own compositions, and Purcell's earliest sonatas are anything but virtuoso works, though his technique advanced by the time he came to write his second set. In sum, we may read into his preface a leaning towards the gravity of the Italian chamber style in general and a revolt from the more superficial dance rhythms of the French instrumental music.

It is noteworthy that to contemporary observers Purcell, and indeed English composers generally, seemed to be holding a middle course between the French and Italian styles. Thus Motteux, the gossiping paragraphist of the 'Gentleman's Journal,' reporting on the 'Fairy Queen,' speaks of the composer as joining 'to the Delicacy and beauty of the Italian way, the Graces and Gayety

of the French.' Purcell had himself, somewhat
earlier, given credence to this idea in the preface
to 'Dioclesian' where he says, with his usual assumption of modesty, 'Musick is yet but in its
nonage, a forward child, which gives hope of what
it may be hereafter in England, when the Masters
of it shall find more Encouragement. 'Tis now
learning Italian, which is its best Master, and
studying a little of the French Air, to give it somewhat more of Gayety and Fashion. Thus being
farther from the sun, we are of later Growth than
our Neighbour Countries and must be content to
shake off our Barbarity by degrees.' Unlike
Locke, and unlike the champions of the English
instrumental school, Purcell was always willing
(perhaps too willing) to admit his susceptibility
to foreign influence. We must, no doubt, dis-
count his words a little in considering that they
were addressed to a ducal patron whose prejudice
would be in favour of the fashionable foreign
schools of the time, as English patronage of the
arts has usually been. But there is no need to
convict Purcell of complete insincerity. He was
not, like Dryden, the man to rail against the
foreigner at the moment when he was proposing
to conform to the taste for foreign gewgaws. He
seems to have been an entirely practical and
open-minded person who was ready to take
the good things where he found them and ever

disposed, like Bach, to accept whatever could be profitably assimilated into his own personal economy. He was, at the same time, far from being uncritical. He lived in a very critical age and the spirit of the age was strong in him.

It was an age, in many respects, of violent contrasts, one which witnessed an ostensible restoration of the old order and at the same time the birth of a new; an inquisitive, adventurous age and one which yet displayed curious reversions to type; an age of prose in which poetasters swarmed; of great preachers and loose morals; an age which could produce on the one hand its Bishop Ken and on the other its vicars of Bray, and could combine the credulity of an Aubrey with the exact investigations of a Newton; which gave rein to the philosophical transactions of the Royal Society and to interminable disquisitions on the casuistry of love; an age that sought to depict itself in heroic attitudes and high-falutin' rhetoric, and produced its true reflection in plain-spoken, anti-romantic comedies; in which a highly urbane society affected to believe in Arcadian simplicities: and while conscious of its own modernity, aped a pseudo-classicism. In music, it was an age at once avid of novelties and apprehensive of them, eager to be thought in the new mode and yet clinging desperately to the old and out-moded. It was, at most points, an age not very unlike our

own, a post-war age, full of national self-consciousness and cosmopolitan affectations. . . .

From the Elizabethan standpoint, it was doubtless a somewhat decadent age, just as from the
Victorian standpoint our own may appear decadent. The mistake lies in measuring the achievements of one age by the ideals of another. Elizabethan lyric poetry and poetic drama seem like
pure gold beside the alloy of the Restoration poets
and playwrights. The age of Nahum Tate and
Shadwell, and even of the greater Dryden, must
rank in its poetic and artistic ideals as definitely
inferior to the age of Shakespeare and Ben Jonson,
and if we approach the music of the Restoration
period from the preconceived angle of the polyphonic school, we may be similarly tempted to
write it down as a sad falling from grace. But
the age of Purcell set itself the task of raising on
the foundation of the past a superstructure of a
totally different kind. Its foremost feature is not
that it either secularised or modernised music,
but that it made music professional and public.
There were, of course, professional musicians and
professional performers in the earlier time and
at all times. But whereas music had in the main
been made by professionals for amateurs, it was
now principally to be made by professionals for
professionals. Even in the sphere of chamber-
music, the last stronghold of the amateur, there

were signs of change in the appearance of the virtuosi and the growth of the public concert. Two things – the opera and the violin – sealed the amateur's fate. He has survived, but only on sufferance.

The view which has usually been taken of the standard of musical taste during the Restoration period has unfortunately been coloured to a large extent by the writings of authors like Mace and Simpson, who were wedded to the old ways and confirmed in the opinion that music was going to the dogs. These special pleaders were not alone in their bewailings. Even an up-to-date and successful publisher like Playford can scarcely put a volume on the market without the customary lament. 'Musick in this age (like other Arts and Sciences) is in low esteem with the generality of people, our late and Solemn Musick, both Vocal and Instrumental, is now justl'd out of esteem by the new Corants and Jigs of Foreigners to the grief of all sober and judicious Understanders of that formerly solid and good Musick.'[1] We sometimes feel, in reading these mournful prefaces, some faint sympathy with Charles II to whom this solid solemnity of the English – or their pretence to it – was so repugnant. As for the new Corants and Jigs, it was Playford and no other who issued, ten years before the Restoration, his ' English

---

[1] 'Introduction to the Skill of Musick,' 8th Edition 1679.

Dancing Master,' and thus helped to establish the taste for dance rhythms.

But music, contrary to what Playford says, was not at all in low esteem. A typical amateur of the period, like Roger L'Estrange (a 'very musical gentleman and had a tolerable Perfection on the Bass Viol') could bear his part in a Consort at a moment's notice, just like the Elizabethan gentry mentioned by Morley, who sang madrigals at sight. Evelyn, the diarist, dining at Lord Sunderland's or Lord Falkland's has 'rare' music after dinner and hears the celebrated Mr. Pordage, newly come from Rome. Music meetings were sufficiently in vogue to be satirised in the current comedies. True, there were the dilettanti, like Shadwell's Sir Positive At-all, who pretended to more than they understood and made Corants with a 'soul' in them,[1] but the type is not unknown at other periods. Indeed the very frequency of the allusions to music in Restoration comedy prove that those allusions were likely to be appreciated at their worth. Modern playwrights cannot afford to venture into regions in which neither they nor the bulk of their audience are at home.[2] That music was practised in the country

[1] A caricature of Sir Robert Howard, the dramatist, whose wife was a favourite pupil of Purcell.

[2] There is an amusing scene in 'The Maid's Last Prayer' (Southerne) in which Sir Symphony, a 'fanatico per la musica' conducts a rehearsal :

as well as in London seems likely. Motteux's monthly news-letter invariably contained a musical supplement, in which a new song by Blow, Purcell or other composers of the time was included and the musical events of the day briefly recorded. Clerical musicians like the versatile Dean Aldrich of Christ Church or Robert Creyghton of Wells and many others were themselves composers and patrons of the art. Music, in short, flourished.

Patronage, though it could, on occasion, show a niggardly spirit, was fairly widespread. Purcell acknowledges it in several places. 'Nothing,' says North, 'advanced musick more in this age than the patronage of the nobility and men of fortune, for they became encouragers of it by great liberallitys and countenance to the professors.' Public concerts, started by the disgruntled Banister in 1672 and developed by Britton, the 'musical small-coal man' six years later, were immediately successful. North tells

'*Sir Symphony*: Come, pray, let's begin [All the while the symphony plays, he beats time and speaks in admiration of it] O Gad: there's a flat note ! there's art ! how surprisingly the key changes ! o law ! there's a double relish ! I swear, sir, you have the sweetest little finger in England ! ha ! that stroke's new; I tremble every inch of me; now ladies, look to your hearts – softly, gentlemen – remember the echo – captain, you play the wrong tune – o law ! my teeth ! my teeth ! for God's sake, captain, mind your cittern – Now the fuga, bases ! again, again ! lord ! Mr. Humdrum, you come in three bars too soon. Come, now the song.' – The song is Purcell's 'Tho' you make no return to my passion.'

us of a musical coterie that met to listen privately to performances on the violin and was compelled to give up its meetings because the pressure of demand for admission became too great, whereupon the musicians carried on by themselves with such good success that they were soon able to take over a newly built concert-room. It is not unbelievable that the tone of these fashionable meetings was at first somewhat low and that 'musical curiosities' and variegated programmes were the rule. Britton's concerts seem, however, to have set a higher standard and he managed to attract most of the leading musicians of the time.

But the most significant feature of the Restoration music was its steady invasion of the public theatres. Music from the time of Shakespeare had always had its place in the drama. No picture of English manners, however it might be disguised in romantical settings, was complete unless it included the practice of music, which was so prominent a factor in English domestic life. But from the time of the Restoration, music, which had traditionally been an accessory, designed to create atmosphere or give point to dramatic moods, and reserved for occasions of ritual, pageantry or supernaturalism, began to assume an alarming preponderance. In the masques it had still in the main been subsidiary.

In the spectacular shows of the Restoration it assumed major proportions. The compromising English talent invented a form which was neither opera nor play, but a pastiche of both (which Roger North aptly called 'Ambigues' or semi-operas) and excused itself on the pretence that 'two good dishes were better than one.'[1] While the characteristic Italian form was the lyric opera and the characteristic French form the opera-ballet, the English developed the type of play with music which has since remained its most beloved entertainment. Its ancestor was the masque; its progeny the musical comedies and spectacular reviews of our time. It is useless to lament, as many writers have done, that this particular form is neither flesh, nor fowl nor good red herring. It happens to be a peculiarly English form of amusement. Purcell's main work cannot be understood unless we frankly accept it.

In vain did the writers of the Restoration era protest against the inroads of music and spectacle on the sacred preserves of the drama. And they were no doubt right in attributing the decay of a purely dramatic art to the introduction of scenic splendour and musical fripperies. 'It was no wonder,' says Colley Cibber, 'that this sensual supply of sound and sight grew too hard for sense and simple nature, when it is considered how

[1] 'A fond mistake,' adds North.

many more people there are that can see and hear than can think and judge. So wanton a change of the public taste, therefore, began to fall heavy upon the King's company [the legitimate theatre] and of the encroachment upon wit several good prologues in those days complained.' The prologues (or if not, the epilogues) were certainly very severe, and with the usual English aptitude for adopting a high moral tone while in the act of giving the public what it wants, Shadwell is able to say, at the conclusion of his garbled version of the 'Tempest':—

> When you of witt, and sence, were weary growne,
> Romantick, riming, fustian plays were showne.
> We then to flying witches did advance,
> And for your pleasures traffick'd into ffrance.
> From thence new arts to please you, we have sought,
> We have machines to some perfection brought,
> And about thirty warbling voyces gott.

In vain did Dryden theorise as to the proper functions of opera and declaim against 'murdering Plays, which they miscal Reviving'; in vain did the farce-writer Duffett produce his amusingly scurrilous burlesques of the Dorset Garden shows. The 'decorated nonsense and pantomimical trumpery' won the day.

At the very least these things enjoyed an enormous vogue. No doubt their success in many instances was more apparent than real, for the huge costs of production, with the lavish settings and double casts of actors and singers which the semi-operas entailed, must have demanded packed houses during the comparatively short runs of those days, if the expenses were to be recouped. Nor can we always take the lamentations of the legitimate dramatists, as expressed in their pessimistic prologues, at the face value. The topical prologue of the day with its gibes at the wits and the witless, its railings at 'scenes, machines and empty operas' became, indeed, a conventional formality. The dramatists might profess to be seriously alarmed, and then, as now, there were theatrical Cassandras who were ready to take the gloomiest view of the future of the drama, but it was the craze for adaptations which set the example of butchering plays to make an operatic holiday, and it was satire rather than spectacle that killed the heroic play. Opera flourished on heroics and was, as Dryden astutely perceived, their logical outcome. The Apostasy from Sense produced the Idolatry of Sound. 'For when we complain,' says Cibber (whose phrase this is) 'that the finest musick, purchas'd at such a vast Expense is so often thrown away upon the most miserable Poetry; we seem not to consider that when the movement of the Air and Tone of the Voice are exquisitely harmonised, tho' we regard not one word of what we hear, yet the Power of the melody is so busy in the Heart, that we naturally annex Ideas to it of our own Creation, and in some sort become our selves the Poet to the Composer.'

Dryden, when he finally surrendered himself to Purcell, was quick to observe, with his customary adaptability, that when poetry met music, it was an affair of give-and-take, in which the music did most of the taking. And in the preface to 'King Arthur,' he makes a very interesting apology for his text. 'There is nothing,' he says, 'better than what I intended, but the music; which has since arrived to a greater perfection in *England* than ever formerly, especially passing through the artful hands of Mr. *Purcel*, who has compos'd it with so great a genius, that he has nothing to fear but an ignorant, ill-judging Audience. But the Numbers of Poetry and Vocal Musick are sometimes so contrary, that in many places I have been obliged to cramp my Verses, and make them rugged to the Reader, that they may be harmonious to the Hearer. Of which I have no Reason to repent me, because these sorts of Entertainment are principally designed for the Ear and Eye.' This, although somewhat grudgingly expressed, is quite a fair statement of the function of the librettist. Dryden might, indeed, have been content to leave the matter in the hands of Purcell, whose skill in setting all kinds of words, poetic or otherwise, he must have recognised as supreme. As it was, he was possibly a little piqued at being forced into playing second fiddle to a musical genius, who at the same time did not scruple to cut his verses, when he found them superfluous to the musical design. The poor librettist never gets much credit, anyhow. But it says something for Dryden's practical nature that he so frankly acknowledges the claims of music.

It is doubtful if in any other period English poets have made so serious an effort to write words for music. The result may not always be fine poetry, and in fact it is Dryden's plea that fine poetry in the absolute sense is not what music, at any rate operatic music, requires. Dryden's is, indeed, almost the only name, in the history of English opera of a serious type, that has lent any dignity to the tribe of hacks, scribblers and versifiers who have made the literature of the operatic 'book' a byword. His lyrics often contain flat lines, tedious inversions, and drab images, such as are the common fault of operatic verse. But, a first class literary technician, he does seem to have felt that a special kind of technique was required for this class of work and to have studied to produce a serviceable instrument. And he is often remarkably successful. It is more than likely that in this he received some suggestions from Purcell – he half admits as much. Purcell himself, in the prefatory dedication to 'Dioclesian,' which finally brought over Dryden to his side, had already remarked that the poets 'begin to grow asham'd of their harsh and broken Numbers, and promise to file our uncouth Language into smoother Words' – perhaps with the memory of Nahum Tate, his collaborator in 'Dido,' fresh in his mind.

Never were the prospects of a purely English form of musical-dramatic entertainment brighter than at this moment, the purely English being a slightly impure amalgam of native tradition, foreign example, and talented compromise. Dryden himself was quite clear in his own mind that the story of an opera must be wholly sung, but the ill-success of 'Albion and Albanius,' the realisation that the English did not take kindly to recitative, to say nothing of the fact that a wholly sung opera tended to depreciate the position of the poet, all pointed to the conclusion that it would be courting failure to try to impose on the English public a type of art for which they were apparently unready and perhaps constitutionally unfitted. Dryden might profess that 'he could not, by the nicest scrutiny get any just Light, either as to the time, or the first Inventers of Operas.'[1] But he seems to have had a very good idea of what constituted opera, though the origins of the form it took in

[1] According to James Relph, author of 'The Touch-Stone' (1728) quoted by Mr. Montague Summers in the introduction to his edition of Dryden's 'Dramatick Works.'

England may have seemed more complex. In essentials it ante-dated the Italian and French operas and its ancestry was to be sought in the masque. In practice, it grafted on the heroic play the quasi-mythological treatment and supernaturalism which was so necessary to the exploitation of the new scenic devices, always however showing signs of a throw-back to the masque.

English conservatism was as strong in the theatre as in music, and the moment was propitious for an attempt to build an English opera on the foundations of the classical English drama and of national legend. Shakespeare was the hinterland of the Restoration stage. Heroic plays were its foreground. Here was all the stuff and material out of which operas are made. Literary purists may exclaim in horror against the complacency with which the Restoration playwrights undertook to improve Shakespeare – at least it must be conceded to them that they seem to have known their job, if we may judge by the continued popularity of their efforts for the best part of a century to come. But opera has no literary scruples to plead. A version of 'The Tempest' such as Davenant made with the approval and help of Dryden, in which Miranda has a twin-sister, Ariel and Caliban female counterparts, and in which a man who has never seen a woman is brought in to off-set the woman who has never seen a man (except her father) may revolt literary susceptibilities, but there have been far worse things done in the name of opera. Unfortunately these things were not done in the name of opera but simply as being 'good theatre' and equally unfortunately English opera was not a frank and conscious development but a side-issue, brought on the stage fortuitously, first to disguise plays and then to help mend them. Plays, indeed, the so-called 'Drammatick Operas' remained, with music and spectacle making gradually deeper incisions into the action.

English 'opera,' if we can trust Cibber, was born of Fashion out of Necessity. At the Restoration, or shortly after, there were two theatrical companies in London. One, the King's Company, under Tom Killigrew, was installed in the house which afterwards became famous as the Theatre Royal, Drury Lane. It was destroyed by fire early in 1672 and two years later a new theatre designed by Wren was opened. It was here that Dryden spoke the prologue we have already quoted and that the more serious and traditional drama was cultivated. It was undoubtedly an age of great actors and many of the plays which seem flat and uninspired in print became magnificent in the mouths of the Restoration players. The other company was maintained under the patent granted to Sir William Davenant, whose 'Siege of Rhodes' four years before the Restoration had

been a small-scale effort[1] to test the indulgence
of the authorities towards a stage-entertainment
that avoided being a play. Davenant's company,
after various moves, opened the handsome new
theatre in Dorset Gardens in 1671 and on his death
it was carried on by the actors Harris and Betterton. This house was largely devoted to spectacular
productions, and the rivalry of the two companies
was keen. There was in fact a ding-dong battle
for public favour. Betterton was himself the leading Shakespearean actor of the time and one of
the greatest of all times, but on the whole the
King's Company seems to have been held in
higher repute for its acting. Cibber, indeed, says
that it was in order to cope with the success of the
rival house that Davenant, after the Restoration,
took to music and spectacle. The balance immediately swung over to the Dorset Gardens shows,
with such productions as Locke's 'Psyche' on
which over £800 was spent (a large sum in those
days[2]) and the mutilated 'Tempest.' Burlesques
and stunt productions with entirely female casts
failed to retrieve the fortunes of the King's men,
until in 1682, on Killigrew's death, the two companies were amalgamated and the patentees, having

---

[1] 'A contracted Trifle as that of the Caesars carv'd upon a
Nut,' as Davenant described it.

[2] Though nothing like the colossal amounts that were expended
on the masques. Shirley's 'Masque of Peace' prepared by the
Inns of Court in 1634 cost £21,000.

a monopoly of stage-productions, were able to exercise economies at the expense of the actors and to keep the spheres of the two theatres distinct. It was at Dorset Gardens that many of Purcell's larger works were produced.

It will help us to understand the atmosphere in which Purcell worked if we pay an imaginary visit to the Duke's theatre on a May afternoon in 1674. Having come to see the show rather than ogle the ladies from the stage boxes, we shall take our place in the already crowded and not too comfortable pit. The hour is 3.30. The play is 'The Tempest, or The Enchanted Island,' as made into an opera by Mr. Shadwell, 'having all new in it, as Scenes, Machines etc.' The music has been written by Mr. Locke with the assistance (in the vocal numbers) of Mr. Pelh. Humfrey and Mr. Banister. The orchestra has been specially augmented for the occasion by members of the King's band of violins and his Majesty has been pleased to give instructions that 'Mr. Turner and Mr. Hart or any other men or boys belonging to his Majesty's Chappell Royal that sing in the Tempest at His Royal Highnesse Theatre doe remaine in towne all the weeke (during his Majesty's absense from Whitehall) to performe that service, only Saturdayes to repaire to Windsor and to returne to London on Mundayes if there be occasion for them. And that they also performe the like service in the opera in the said theatre or any other thing in the like nature where their helpe may be desired upon notice given thereof.' Among these Chapel Royal choristers, whose week is so pleasantly mapped out between the rival claims of the church and the theatre, the young man Purcell is not included, for his voice has recently broken, but it is possible that he is somewhere in the house to hear his friend Locke's new music. Poor Mr. Humfrey, who is no doubt present to direct the singers and perhaps conduct the band, is making one of the last public appearances of his brief and brilliant career.[1]

And now 'the Front of the Stage is open'd, and the band of 24 violins, with the Harpsicals and Theorbo's which accompany the voices, are plac'd between the Pit and Stage. While the Overture is playing, the Curtain rises and discovers a new Frontispiece, joined to the great Pilasters, on each side of the Stage. This Frontispiece is a Noble Arch, supported by large wreathed Columns of the Corinthian Order; the wreathings of the Columns are beautifi'd with Roses wound round them and several Cupids flying about them. On the Cornice, just over the Capitals, sits on either side a Figure, with a trumpet in one hand, and a Palm in the other, representing Fame. A little farther on the same Cornice, on each side of a

---

[1] He died two months later at Windsor.

Compass-Pediment, lie a Lion and a Unicorn, the supporters of the Royal Arms of England. In the middle of the Arch are several Angels, holding the King's Arms, as if they were placing them in the midst of that Compass-Pediment. Behind this is the Scene, which represents a thick Cloudy Sky, a very Rocky Coast, and a Tempestuous sea in perpetual Agitation. This Tempest (suppos'd to be raised by Magic) has many Dreadful Objects in it, as several Spirits in horrid shapes flying amongst the Sailers, then rising and crossing in the Air. And when the ship is sinking the whole House is darken'd, and a shower of Fire falls upon 'em. This is accompanied by Lightning and several Claps of Thunder to the end of the Storm.' But even these scenic wonders are eclipsed by the back-cloths 'painted with myriads of Ariel spirits,'[1] the pantomime transformations, flying devils, dancing Winds, Neptune in a Chariot drawn by Sea-Horses, a ballet of Trytons, and a final tableau of the Rising Sun. Well might Alonzo remark: 'O Heavens ! yet more Apparitions !'

It was for this theatre, with its Shakespearean improvements, and its *décor*, like that tempestuous sea, in perpetual agitation, that Purcell wrote his most enchanting music. Literary historians, seeing the whole thing through the decayed formulae of a bad literary tradition, have written it off as

[1] Downes, 'Roscius Anglicanus.'

ludicrous. But it is no more ludicrous than a description of the scenic appliances of Wagner's operas will seem to readers two hundred years hence. So far from its being necessary for the salvage of Purcell's music to remove it from the historical context, we cannot properly understand it except in relation to the wreathed columns, flying Cupids, devils and witches, plumes of feathers and fantastic appurtenances of the Restoration theatre. He was an immensely professional composer writing for an immensely professional stage. It is one of the most singular ironies that he should have become almost exclusively the preserve of amateurs. Yet it is certain that if his work is to be re-created in the style in which he conceived it, the efforts of amateurs will not suffice. It is only by production on some vast Cochranesque scale that we can place his music in anything like an appropriate setting.

Purcell's music for the stage falls into two groups – that which was written for revivals and that which was composed for original productions. Much confusion has been caused by the assignment of dates to his dramatic works in accordance with the original productions of plays for which only at a later revival was he called in to write incidental music or which were subsequently converted into 'drammatick operas.' The trend of public taste during the latter part of his life was predominantly in the direction of musical entertainments. Purcell, reaping the benefit of the more tentative efforts of his immediate fore-runners, was engaged to make new settings of works which had already won popularity at the hands of other composers. Even plays in which there was very little excuse for music, were tricked out with songs and dances by the most popular composer of the day. We see him turning his hand to this apparently trivial but not unprofit-able task, to the point of becoming the theatrical composer in ordinary of the later Restoration period. It has been lamented that he threw away the treasures of his genius on so many ephemeral objects. The fact that these plays were not so ephemeral as they now seem but were constantly revived during the next century and very often with Purcell's music, has been largely ignored. The taste of the Restoration audiences is often regarded as deplorable, but vast as were the quantities of music that Purcell composed for the theatre, there are very few signs of slovenly workmanship or hasty production. There has been no English theatre-music since to compare with Purcell's, which preserves even in its lightest moments not merely the supreme quality of fitness for its purpose, but a sterling musical integrity. The musical taste of a period which accepted and delighted in this music cannot have been so deplorable as we are frequently led to suppose.

From the date of his first collaboration with Dryden Purcell's music for the theatre begins to assume an importance that outweighs that of his work in other fields. The turning point had been 'Dioclesian,' his answer to the pretensions of Monsieur Grabu. He was now in his thirty-second year and had five more years to live. As with so many composers who have died at a comparatively early age, these last years give the impression of having been crowded with feverish activity – it is probably an illusion, for Purcell was by no means a spent force at his death. There is no indication of declining powers of invention or exhausted inspiration in his last works. On the contrary, in spontaneity of utterance and in fertility of resource they are unexcelled by anything he ever wrote. In these five years he wrote incidental music for some forty plays besides the four quasi-operatic masterpieces 'King Arthur,' 'The Fairy Queen,' 'The Indian Queen' and 'The Tempest.' In the meantime, he was writing, year by year, ceremonial and occasional Odes; he was still organist at Westminster Abbey where he was to produce the last and most moving of his anthems, on the death of Queen Mary – a few months before his own death; and for the St. Cecilia celebration of 1694 he produced one of his most ambitious choral works, the 'Te Deum and Jubilate.' He was, even more than Elgar in our day, the musician-laureate of his period and though he shared with Blow and others the task of writing the pomp-and-circumstantial music of his time, none of his contemporaries seem to have left so deep an impression on the public consciousness. 'I appeal to all that were present,' says the enthusiastic Dr. Tudway, speaking of the Queen Mary Funeral Anthem, 'as well such as understood music, as those that did not, whether they ever heard anything so rapturously fine and solemn, and so heavenly in the operation, which drew tears from all; and yet a plain natural composition, which shows the power of music, when 'tis rightly fitted and adapted to devotional purposes.'

Purcell's music was always 'rightly fitted and adapted' to whatever was the purpose of the occasion. The charge of being an 'occasional' composer or poet is one which is apt to have depressing associations in a country that has not always been too fortunate in those on whom the official laurels have been placed. But it is a charge which would have seemed completely meaningless in an age when practically all music was written for immediate use and when performance rather than publication was the end in sight. And Purcell shows himself a completely unselfconscious composer whether he is writing a 'Yorkshire Feast' song, an Ode on the happy return of His Majesty from Newmarket, a song for a birthday celebration, or an anthem for a royal funeral. Even when he is confronted with the empty bombast and servile flatteries of some of the royal odes, his art is never demeaned and rarely sounds forced. We have to bear in mind the enormous popularity of the monarchy at the Restoration, in order to account for the tone of these royal addresses and for the complaisance with which Purcell put his hand to much that was deplorable as poetry. Loyalty to the constitution, whatever happened to be constitutional, was capable of inspiring sentiments of quite unaffected sincerity. The source of the inspiration mattered less than the idea represented, whether the occasion was one of rejoicing or solemnity, and for the 'gloomy and fanatical' James II Purcell could write some of his most eloquent music. He never failed to rise to a great ceremonial opportunity. His whole career was made up of such opportunities and his essentially dramatic genius passed easily from the theatre in Dorset Gardens to the theatre of public life.

We can see how his fame came to be linked inseparably with those great public occasions for which he triumphantly provided the music. He is the first of our festival composers and his music demands the ceremonial atmosphere. We can see, too, how it was that he became something of a legend in his own generation and why he has remained something of a legend ever since. He wrote for events which in the nature of things were unique, and after their overwhelming effect had passed away there was no call for a public repetition of the music. He wrote for a stage devoted to entertainments that had no set form and which employed music as a decorative accessory and threw it aside with the rest of the scenery when it had served its purpose. It was only for the chamber that he wrote music that was complete and self-contained. His incidental songs can be detached from their context but are much better in it. A comparatively small proportion of his best work was known to his contemporaries through the medium of the printed score. His ventures into publication seem to have been uniformly unprofitable and towards the latter part of his life he apparently gave up all efforts in this direction. For nearly two centuries he remained famous but largely unpublished, and his fame rested on a relatively small stock of works presented in a form that often left much to be desired. To this day there is no complete edition of his music. That he was not indifferent to the preservation of his work is clear from the care with which he transcribed and revised it, and from the pains he took, on the few occasions when he ventured into print, to present it in an authentic form. Shortly after his death an anthology of his vocal music was issued and the 'beauties of Purcell' became traditional. He has remained the easiest of all composers to anthologise and one of the most troublesome to see whole.

PART TWO

THE MUSIC

'Cannot we put ourselves in loco of former states and judge pro tunc?'

THE HON. ROGER NORTH

CHAPTER I

ELEMENTS OF STYLE

IN the year 1694 there was published a new
edition of John Playford's 'Introduction to
the Skill of Musick.' Honest John, as his contemporaries called him, was a successful popular
publisher whose 'English Dancing Master' (1651)
had lightened the gloom of the Commonwealth,
and has since become the bible of English folk-
dancers. This issue (the twelfth) of his famous
text-book, which ran into a score of editions down
to 1730, had a peculiar virtue: it was edited by
Henry Purcell.[1] The 'Introduction,' designed
for amateurs, included chapters on the theory of
music, singing, and composition, herein described
as the 'Art of Descant, or composing Musick in
Parts.' It was this last section that was revised
by Purcell. For the moment, however, we are
concerned with the chapter on singing which, it
is to be noted, Purcell or Playford Junior was
content to reprint as it stood.

[1] The previous editors had been Thomas Campion and Christopher Simpson. The section on composition, originally written
by Campion, was replaced by a new treatise in the 10th edition
(1683) but the 12th edition seems to be the first to which Purcell's
name can with certainty be attached.

In this chapter, the author who is professed to be 'an English Gentleman who had long lived in Italy and being returned Taught the same here' – the 'same' being the Italian manner of singing – inveighs against the practice of composing divisions, or gracings, on the melody. 'Those long windings and turnings of the voice' he says, 'are ill-used; for I have observed that Divisions have been invented, not because they are necessary to the good fashion of singing, but rather for a certain tickling of the ears of those who do not well understand what it is to sing passionately; for if they did, undoubtedly Divisions would have been abhorred, there being nothing more contrary to passion than they are.' The English ideal of art as being simple, sensuous and passionate seems to be vindicated out of the mouth of Italy.

It is probable however, that the professions of the English Gentleman who had long lived in Italy were slightly dishonest, in so far as he himself did not exist but was an invention of the fertile imagination of the publisher. The essay seems, indeed, not to have been based on personal experience but to have been largely borrowed from the preface to Caccini's 'Nuove Musiche' (1602) the manifesto of the new recitative style. Caccini had complained, in very similar terms, of the growing habit among singers of introducing florid passages, more suited to wind or stringed instruments than to the human voice, and of their abuses of expression and ornaments. To combat this tendency he gave elaborate instructions as to the method in which the new music was to be sung and indicated such graces as were to be permitted.[1]

The first begetters of dramatic recitative had proposed to themselves the aim of a just and intelligent declamation of the poetry. Such an ideal, pleasing enough to amateurs whose interest in the new art was at least as much literary as musical, was bound to find itself in conflict with the instincts of professional singers, especially in a country which had a brilliant vocal tradition and which even in its ecclesiastical music had developed a type of florid expression that successive decrees of the church authorities had failed to eradicate. In the secular field of opera such checks as the church might impose on its own singers were wanting, and it is not surprising to find that the history of the next hundred years is a record of the long struggle between composers and singers, in which each sought to obtain the upper hand, the composers writing down their requirements at length and the singers missing no

[1] These included the *gruppo*, a simple trill with a termination, another species of trill consisting of rapid repetitions of the same note (*martellato*) and various forms of the *messa di voce* (swelling and diminishing the tone).

opportunity to add their own embellishments and
finally emerging completely triumphant in the
18th century. Long after Caccini's protest
Lully is found fighting a similar battle in France,
this time not only against the singers but also
against instrumentalists, whose passion for divisions and embroideries on the written note
evoked the wrath of that domineering composer.

The force of the instrumental example was
perhaps not less influential on the style of singing
than the singers' own instinct for display. Much
has been made of the descent of the instrumental
music of the early 17th century from vocal
polyphony. The English madrigal composers, it is
true, had in some few instances issued works under
the accommodating formula of being 'apt for
voyces or viols.' Polyphony was in its origin a
vocal art and when transferred to instruments,
especially stringed instruments, it was inevitable
that it should tend at first to copy the singing
characteristics of voices. What is no less certain
is that, as soon as it began fairly to develop,
instrumental style tended to diverge from a purely
vocal style and in turn to react upon it. Throughout the 17th century these interactions are
traceable, tending to produce a vocal style that
borrowed much from instrumental practice, such
as the 'divisions' of the string instruments and
even the graces of the keyboard instruments, and

an instrumental style that owed some of its features to the expressive cantilena of the voice.

Vocal style, it may be said, is normally a plain style, in so far as it is concerned with the delivery of words. Ornaments are from this angle excrescences. Instrumental style, on the contrary, rejoices in ornamental features, which are integral to it. Vocal style proceeds normally by cautious intervals: instrumental style is more agile, preferring runs, leaps, graces and divisions. The voice adopts the methods of instruments only when it dispenses with words and reduces them to the mere function of vocables, or when it aims at realistic suggestions. This classification becomes less rigid, however, as the two styles develop side by side and by being used in association, become mutually imitative. The forms of music are an abstract property which are not confined to one particular medium of expression. In origin, or at a given period, they may appear more native to one particular medium, e.g. the aria form may seem to belong especially to the voice or the variation form to the keyboard. In the process of being transferred to a new medium they retain some of the characteristics of their origin and develop others more peculiar to the adopted medium. Even dance forms, which are by nature instrumental, are transferred to the voice, just as vocal forms are transferred to instruments.

There are thus no pure forms in the sense of there being forms that belong to one medium and no other. The sonata and the fugue, in which instrumental music reaches its highest development, each derive something from vocal precedents.

The trend of vocal music during the 17th century was towards an increasingly ornate style, coinciding with the growing taste for decoration in the plastic arts. This was due partly to the reactions of the instrumental example impinging on vocal style and partly to the emergence of the professional singer. The singer, indeed, became the foremost virtuoso of the time and the cantata for solo voice bore much the same relation to virtuoso interest as does the pianoforte or violin concerto of later date. In England it seems probable that the instrumental style was in advance of the vocal, in point of development, during the first half of the century, and the suppression of the church choirs together with the ban on public theatres, which for the time delayed the introduction of opera, further diverted music into instrumental channels. It was not until the Restoration brought about the re-opening of the theatres and the re-organisation of the Chapel Royal under Captain Cooke that a new impulse was given to the cultivation of singing. Cooke was reported to be 'the best singer, after the

Italian manner, of any in England.'[1] He had been on the stage and it is to be inferred that his singing inclined to the dramatic style. The 'Italian Manner' was presumably the declamatory style of recitative, though it may have been used loosely for the expressive style of vocalisation which was being developed by the Italian schools of singing. Such influence as Humfrey brought to bear as the result of his experiences abroad would serve to reinforce the tendency towards expressive declamation. In the early anthems of Purcell, written for the Chapel Royal, we find many traces of this declamatory influence. The 'verse' anthem, in which passages for the solo voices alternated with passages for full choir, was not, indeed, a novelty. Byrd and Gibbons had written verse-anthems. But the Restoration anthems pushed much further the development of expressive solo writing and even in the characteristic combination of alto, tenor, and bass voices, evolved a style that can only be described as a kind of multiple recitative in which the voices entered in imitation but were not seriously developed on contrapuntal lines. This style was eminently picturesque. It follows the sense of the words and misses no opportunity for literal illustration. Whatever its fitness as a vehicle for the expression of religious sentiments may have been, there can be no doubt that it was an

[1] Evelyn, Diary, 28th Nov. 1654.

admirable school for a composer who was marked out for a dramatic career. Purcell's dramatic music was built on the foundations of the Chapel Royal anthem.

It is not necessary to refer the whole style of expressive singing to the innovations of Humfrey. Captain Cooke was old enough to have inherited something of the Elizabethan tradition. The essential feature of Purcell's style, in his religious and dramatic music alike, was a tendency to illustrate the immediate verbal imagery. An exactly similar tendency is observable in madrigal technique. Thomas Morley had already laid it down in his famous treatise, that vocal music must follow the sense of the words. 'If the subject be light, you must cause your musick to go in motions, which carry with them a celeritie or quickness of time, as minimes, crotchets, and quavers ; if it be lamentable, the note must go in slow and heavy motions, as semibriefs, briefs, and such like. . . . Moreover you must have a care that when your matter signifieth ascending, high heaven and such like, you make your musick ascend: and by the contrarie where your dittie speaks of descending, lowness, depth, hell and others such, you must make your musick descend. For as it will bee thought a great absurditie to talke of heaven and point downward to the earth: so it will be counted great incongruity if a musician upon the words he ascended into heaven should cause his musick to descend. . . . We must also have a care so to applie the notes to the wordes as in singing there be no barbarisme committed: that is, that we cause no syllable which is by nature short, to be expressed by many notes, or one long note, nor no long syllable to be expressed with a short note.'

These principles, which may seem to us rather obvious, were exactly those on which Purcell worked and which he carried to unprecedented lengths. The smallest suggestion of verbal imagery would set him off translating his material into terms of musical illustration. It is lamented that some of the texts which he was later to set were of such poor quality, but it is perhaps not so regrettable if we may suppose that the more prosaic words of much of his secular music served to check an excess of literalism and the production of a musical equivalent of the literary 'conceits' of the Elizabethan writers. His music became increasingly decorative as time went on, but its decoration grew less fragmentary and more organic in a specifically musical sense. Yet the early habit of pictorial treatment never altogether left him and the recurrence of the same images was apt to invite recourse to a stereotyped vocabulary, such as the apparently inevitable dotted notes with which he signalised the emotions of joy, praise or triumph, the pathetic downward slur over the interval of a fourth or fifth which the expression of tenderness in any form rarely failed to evoke, the use of ascending or descending scale passages which the analogies of physical movement invariably suggested. These processes were not peculiar to Purcell. They were part of the traditional and current vocabulary of music. They stand out in Purcell's music by reason of their frequency and their characteristic emphasis. They are not so much clichés as habits of thought, acquired habits possibly, but so assimilated as to become quite personal. A great composer is not afraid of conventions. It is only the uninspired who studiously avoid them or invent careful paraphrases of the obvious.

Purcell's imagination could scarcely fail to be fired by the Old Testament texts of his Chapel Royal anthems, with their highly coloured images and picturesque suggestions. Confronted with the words 'Like them that go down into the pit,' he writes a bass solo with descending scale passages of over an octave, reaching double D at the repetition of the phrase (the Reverend John Gostling had an exceptionally fine bass voice). Or, if he has to express the sentiment of falling away from the divine grace, he does so by wide downward leaps in all the parts. In the anthem 'Why do the Heathen,' the kings of the earth 'stand up' to a musical imagery of rising fourths and fifths, and the rulers 'take counsel together' in close thirds which have a curious suggestion of secrecy. In the passage 'Be wise now, therefore, O ye Kings: be learned,' the dramatic use of rests gives an air of arcane mystery to the music.[1] But Purcell could be more subtle than this. No feature of the Restoration anthems has been so severely criticised as the refrains of 'gabbling Alleluias' (as Parry called them) which terminate so many of these songs of praise. Purcell certainly praised God with a cheerful voice and he rings the changes on the word 'Alleluia' with a variety of accent that even Handel did not equal in his famous chorus. But in the anthem 'I will give thanks unto Thee, O Lord,' there are, strangely enough, no Alleluias. Yet the whole work is coloured by an instrumental figure which has clearly an alleluia effect.[2]

(All - e - lui - a!)

Other details are more obvious. 'For though the Lord be *high*, yet hath he respect unto the *lowly*' –

[1] Curiously anticipating the trio at the end of the first act of Mozart's 'Magic Flute,' where the genii exhort Tamino, in similar admonitory phrases, broken by rests, to be steadfast, patient, and to 'use discretion.'

[2] It is, for instance, identical in shape and rhythm with the setting of the word 'Hallelujah' in the early 'Elegy on the Death of Matthew Locke.' (1677), and in the Anthem 'My Beloved Spake.'

a descent of two octaves. 'As for the proud he beholdeth them *afar off*' – the voice leaps from one extreme of register to the other.

These devices may seem a trifle puerile. But they were part and parcel of the musical system under which Purcell grew up. He refined upon them but he never entirely forsook them. Music for him, as it may be granted the best English music has generally been, was not a self-contained art, though he could, when occasion demanded, write works of pure abstract beauty such as the Fantasies and Sonatas for violins. But chiefly it was an expressive, poetic art, even an accessory art, an art of illustration rather than of abstract design. Towards the end of his life he enlarged his sense of design and wrote works which, even in the vocal sphere, bear more than a casual resemblance to the vast frescoes of Handel. But the illustrative principle remained strong in him and he did not so much abandon it, in adapting a less obviously descriptive style, as raise it to the degree of elaborate metaphor. Throughout his career he was capable of writing realistic passages, such as the following, taken respectively from the anthem 'Why do the Heathen' (c. 1682–85) and the 'Indian Queen,' one of his very last works.

laugh ———————— them to — scorn.

pants ——————————————————— for breath

The realistic suggestion is obvious and on paper it looks a good deal more disconcerting than it would sound in the mouth of a brilliant bass singer, such as Gostling or Leveridge.[1] Purcell, it must be insisted, was an immensely professional composer writing for immensely professional singers. Without the brilliance of execution which his florid music pre-supposed, it is apt to fall to pieces or sound merely trivial. There is no composer to whom we may liken him, under this aspect, more closely than Liszt, whose songs, in their attention to immediate detail, are in the line of the Purcellian 'scena,' and whose style demands a similar virtuosity of treatment, as all art that relies on an elaboration of detail inevitably must.

Nothing could be more misleading, from the point of view of Purcell's style, than to ignore this decorative element. The image of Purcell as the composer of innocent little tunes to which the adjectives pure, limpid, healthy or direct are

[1] Richard Leveridge (1670–1758) chiefly remembered as the composer of 'All in the Downs' and 'The Roast Beef of Old England' was one of the most famous singers of the day. He appeared in several of Purcell's 'operas' and retained his vocal powers till the middle of the next century. The song from which the second extract is taken ('Ye twice ten hundred Deities') was written for him.

sometimes applied, is woefully incomplete. No composer ever had a greater flow of spontaneous melody. The stream runs in places over the shallows just as it elsewhere finds its translucent depths. But these are not the only features of its course. There are 'long windings and turnings' which cannot be charted on the principles of Playford's treatise. Purcell's vocal music is based on the vocal practice of the time. He was himself a celebrated singer. We have a specimen of his methods in the air ' 'Tis Nature's Voice' which occurs in the 'Ode on St. Cecilia's Day' (1692) and which contemporary report said was sung 'with incredible graces by Mr. Purcell himself.' The graces are perhaps even more incredible on paper. Dr. Burney described this air as 'an enigmatical song, seemingly on Music, in which Purcell has crowded all the fashionable passages of taste and vocal difficulty of the times. Indeed he seems to have anticipated many fantastical feats of execution and articulation in which the great performers have since rioted; and this is the more wonderful, as the Italian opera was not established or even attempted here during the life of Purcell.'[1]

Burney evidently thought the taste of these passages questionable, for he calls Purcell's florid melodies 'obsolete and uncouth, from the temporary graces with which he overloaded them,

[1] The latter part of this sentence is not perhaps strictly true.

for the sake of ignorant singers; and indeed he wrote for no other.' These 'furbelows and flounces' required to be removed in the interests of good taste, symmetry and elegance – virtues of the eighteenth century. Modern editors have in certain instances had the same feeling and have followed Burney's advice, both here and in the matter of Purcell's equally ' uncouth' harmonies, by taking out the frills and smoothing out the lines. But this will not do. We cannot improve the style of one period by making it conform to the conventions of another.

Much of what looks like an excess of ornamentation in Purcell's vocal music, however, is nothing more than an attempt to render in notation what the voice actually does in practice. The psychology of notation merits study. It seems fated that when composers write out their intentions in full, an exaggerated importance should be attached to the literal appearance of the notes, and on the contrary when these are represented by conventional signs their significance should be frequently minimised. Purcell very largely adopted the habit of writing out his vocal graces in full. On paper his music seems over-laden with dotted notes, appoggiature, and fioriture, to an extravagant extent. In practice it is found to be based on a sure instinct for vocal effect. Even the dotted notes which stand out so glaringly in the printed page are frequently no more than a method of swinging from point to point, whereas if sung with exaggerated rhythmic emphasis they reduce the music to triviality. The double appoggiatura or upward slur of a third is often a kind of portamento effect, which follows from the natural tendency to secure emphasis by approaching the note from below.

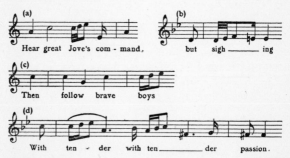

This effort to tell the whole story in written notation was not new. Dr. Fellowes has pointed out that it was sometimes employed by the madrigalists, and Byrd and Gibbons also made use of it in their church music. Some of Purcell's devices of notation, such as the repeated quavers which are intended to secure a shivering effect in the 'Frost Scene' out of 'King Arthur,' were anticipated by earlier composers, like Monteverde and his English pupil Porter. It is odd that in his instrumental music for amateurs, particularly in the harpsichord lessons published after his death by his widow, the ornaments are always represented by conventional signs. These pieces were, however, prefaced by a list of 'Rules for Graces.' Some of the signs, such as the 'forefall' and the 'backfall,' are occasionally used in the vocal music, but more often the graces are written out. There can be no question but that the execution in either case is the same. Christopher Simpson, whose directions are more detailed, divides graces into smooth and shaked, the former applying to stringed instruments and being in the nature of portamenti. And these are precisely the ones which Purcell in his vocal music, as a general rule, wrote out in full.

Purcell's vocal style was based on inflectional principles derived from his Elizabethan predecessors.[1] In his acceptance of the modern major and minor scales he was a less up-to-date composer than Humfrey or even Lawes. He used both scales but he always tended to revert in moments of poignant expression to the simultaneous employment of major and minor tonalities which characterised the work of Byrd and his contemporaries. It has been noticed that the English composers showed signs of breaking away from the old modal system somewhat earlier than composers in other countries, inventing, with the usual English faculty for practical compromises, a

[1] See Miss M. H. Glyn's 'Elizabethan Music and Composers.'

123

system that was neither modal nor scalic in the modern sense. This practice survived down to the time of Purcell, and indeed later. Dr. Cummings quoted the statement of Stafford Smith that 'Mr. Purcell has been heard to declare more than once, that the variety which the minor key is capable of affording by the change of sounds in the ascending and descending scales, induced him so frequently to give it the preference.' Purcell's fondness for the minor mode will be obvious to anyone who glances through the famous collection of his songs called 'Orpheus Britannicus.' But the peculiarities of his style cannot be altogether explained by a simple preference for the melodic minor scale. If we take the well known recitative from 'Dido and Aeneas' we shall find that the matter is rather more subtle and better explained as a combined use of the major and minor third.

dark — - - -ness   shades me

The nominal key of the recitative at the outset is C minor, written, it is to be noticed, with only two flats in the signature. It modulates on the word 'shades' to F minor and the really important feature of the phrase quoted is the alternation of the A natural and A flat as the third of the scale. In Playford's 'Introduction,' Purcell laid down the

general principles of tonality accepted in his time:
'There are but two Keys in musick viz a Flat and
a Sharp; not in relation to the Place where the first
or last Note in the piece of Musick stands, but the
Thirds above the Note.' As for the rest of the
scale it might be inflected in a variety of ways,
often, but not by any means invariably, in accordance with the two forms of the melodic minor
scale. It is obvious that once the inflectional
principle is adopted, it lends itself to endless varia-
tions in the interest of expression. The following
passage from 'The Fatal Hour,' one of Purcell's
most moving songs, will illustrate the method.

Here are many of the characteristic features of
Purcell's vocal style, the downward portamento
on the word 'certain' (fourth bar), the flexing of
the voice in little upward phrases, the unsettled
tonality, the word-painting of the whole-tone passage which descends with such grim foreboding
on the word 'misery,' and the repetition of words
to secure emphasis.

Purcell is said to have derived his preference
for the minor mode from Humfrey. If so, Humfrey must have been a good deal more influenced

by Italian than French models, for his supposed
master Lully shows no such preference. Playford speaks of the 'melancholy or flat key' and
'the sharp or chearful key,' but this crude division of the emotional properties of the two keys
is quite inapplicable to Purcell, many of whose
liveliest tunes are written in the minor. The real
explanation, if any is needed, is that the harmonic
resources of the minor mode at this time lent
themselves to a greater variety of treatment.
Purcell's harmony is always adventurous without
appearing strained, but some of his most daring
flights, or what appear to be such, are derived not
from harmonic experiments but from a perfectly
logical procedure in the movement of the parts, in
accordance with the melodic principles mentioned
above. The chord of the sharp third and flat
sixth which Dr. Burney singled out for special
censure was not even new. It is frequently found
in the works of the madrigalists. Whether Purcell
had any practical acquaintance with these works
is more than doubtful. Madrigal singing had
very largely decayed during the second quarter
of the 17th century but the church music
had in part survived and Purcell's experience as
copyist at Westminster must have made him
thoroughly familiar with the older technique. At
any rate we cannot account for the many striking
similarities between his methods and those of the

polyphonic writers except on the ground that he was familiar with their works.

Purcell's own methods are not a little illuminated by the contribution he made to Playford's treatise. His character is revealed in the direct and businesslike way he approaches the subject, dispensing with those agreeable but long-winded digressions of the older writers of text-books; illustrating, by practical example, how music is made rather than writing many precepts and prohibitions; turning a side-glance on the new Italian methods; quoting Dr. Blow with enthusiasm; putting in a word against pedantry; finally, as an afterthought, making light of the very device in which he himself particularly excelled, composing upon a ground bass, 'a very easy thing to do and requires but little Judgement.'[1] The best way to learn was to 'score much and chuse the best Authors.' He finds that Mr. Simpson's 'Rule in Three Parts for Counterpoint is too strict and destructive to Good Air, which ought to be preferr'd before such Nice Rules.'[2] In writing basses, he counsels the

[1] Dr. Burney described this practice, so much cultivated by Purcell and his English forerunners and Italian contemporaries, by his favourite word of disparagement, 'Gothic.' It was 'an unworthy employment for men possessed of such genius and original resources' and forced Purcell to submit to 'a crude and sometimes a licentious and unwarrantable use of passing notes.'

[2] Purcell adds, in making a correction which, he claims, carries 'more Air and Form in it' that he is sure his way is 'the constant practise of the Italians in all their Musick, either Vocal

avoidance of 'Tautology' (the one cardinal sin) and 'let it be as Formal and Airy as the Treble will admit.' This question of 'Good Air' crops up more than once. It is a feature of his own part-writing which gives it at once a singing quality and a sense of lively motion. Purcell's music never marks time. His basses are incomparable. In several places he incorporates popular tunes, intact or slightly modified, into his bass-part,[1] while his 'grounds,' varying from a simple sequence of descending notes to elaborately worked out melodies of great length, are unsurpassed anywhere for variety and ease of movement.

Purcell's mastery of formal device was, in fact, the necessary corrective to his strongly rhapsodical tendency. The perils of his style lay in the temptation to abandon structure in favour of decorative detail, to improvise picturesque metaphors in place of consistent argument. At the slightest hint of an image, particularly one which

or Instrumental, which I presume ought to be a guide to us.' This presuming on the part of the former 'faithful imitator' of the Italian sonatas is something less than enthusiastic. Matthew Locke, who was the idol of his youth, had already, in his foreword to Simpson's 'Compendium of Practical Musick' (1667) spoken of 'the production of Ayre: which, in my opinion, is the Soul of Musick.'

[1] E.g. 'Lilliburlero' (used as the bass to the Jig in 'The Gordian Knot Untied'), the ballad 'Cold and Raw' (in Queen Mary's Birthday Ode, 1692) and 'Hey Boys, up go we' (Welcome Song, 1686).

suggested physical motion, Purcell would go off on the track of an illustration. Suppose he is confronted with the words:

> Turn then thine eyes upon those glories there
> And catching flames will on thy cheek appear.

It is obvious that it is not so much the underlying sentiment of the words that has caught him in the first instance as the physical gesture of the eyes.[1]

Turn, turn then thine eyes, turn, turn, turn, turn, turn, turn, turn,

turn, turn turn

It is this piecemeal illustration which tends to make his style seem to lack consistency and uniformity. He is often completely at the mercy of single words and will even grotesquely ignore the principal sentiment in devoting attention to irrelevant detail. The very aptness of his word-setting is inclined to betray him occasionally into falsities of poetic interpretation. It is the defect of the rhapsodic style, in which the logic of the ideas is less important than the juxtaposition of striking images.

Nevertheless, music is of all the arts the one in

---

[1] This song actually occurs in the 'Fairy Queen' (the masque of Hymen), where it appears as a duet, but it will serve as an illustration of Purcell's method of word-painting. It must, however, be noticed that much that appears far-fetched in the printed page is entirely appropriate when helped out by the physical action on the stage.

which decorative detail can best be reconciled with the functions of design, the one, indeed, in which the distinction between design and detail is most difficult to draw. An architectural detail once it is stated, is always a detail, but music is capable of absorbing its own details as it proceeds and transforming them into the elements of design. A modern composer would perhaps have seen the song quoted above from the latter end, and treated it emotionally rather than picturesquely. Purcell, having committed himself to the figure suggested by the first word, is faced with the alternative of either maintaining his detail or frankly abandoning it and inventing a new one for the irresistible images that immediately follow. In the earlier stages we feel that he would have had no compunction in throwing over his musical image once it had served its purpose, but this is a late work and instead of giving up his triplets he insists on them and when he comes to the word 'flames' he hurries them on in an ascending sequence, omitting the stationary notes between the 'turns.'

flames

This transformation of one detail into another has produced, in fact, an element of consistency in the design.

It is the merging of the principle of illustration into that of abstract design, not always successfully achieved and in his earlier work often not attempted, that is the most interesting feature of Purcell's development as a composer. Separated into their respective elements these principles may be traced at all stages of his career, in the realistic touches of his declamatory solos, on the one hand, and in the more formal shapes of his strophic songs, such as 'Fairest Isle,' on the other. In his solution of the problem of word-setting Purcell's first concern was for correct accentuation. Compared with his syllabic declamation, the efforts of Lawes to achieve 'just note and accent' seem merely amateurish. Even in his florid writing Purcell rarely falls into errors of taste in his choice of words or syllables for ornamental treatment and though he carried these methods to great lengths, almost Handelian lengths at times in his later works, there is comparatively seldom an absolute want of poetic as well as musical justification in his setting. The decorative excesses of the 17th century were not in this matter nearly as great as those of the 18th century, by which time the musical, or rather the instrumental, principle had largely obtained the upper hand. Purcell strove to shake off the purely deferential attitude to poetry that the literary school of Lawes had tried to foist upon music, and even

in his simplest declamatory settings, such as the
Matthew Locke 'Elegy,' he was able to give a cohe-
rent structure to his music, while paying the most
scrupulous regard to the sense and accentuation
of the text.   In such works it is, indeed, his feeling
for the rhythm and cadences of whole sentences,
his punctuation, stress, and attention to the order
of the ideas which his music serves to enforce, that
evoke admiration, as much as his care for correct
verbal accent.   But he shows a different temper
in his treatment of words in the choral odes and
dramatic works of the later period.   Here the
texts are frequently so flat and uninspired that
they invite scant consideration, and Purcell treats
them merely as so much raw material to be
wrought into the musical texture.   Throughout
his life certain words of comprehensive significance, such as 'all,' 'none,' 'more,' 'thousand,'
and so on, were invariably subjected to repetition.   It was partly due to his dramatic instinct
and partly to the convention of writing extended
movements on a comparatively short text.   It
certainly enabled vocal music to take on a larger
span and to free itself from the restrictive influence of the poetic forms.   Nor is the convention of
much repetition a bad one from the point of view
of mere verbal clarity, though no doubt Purcell
and others carried it to excess at times.   Every
concert-listener knows how fatiguing it is to have

to listen to a whole series of songs set on a strictly syllabic and non-repetitive basis and the modern practice of printing the words in concert programmes tells its own story. The invention of refrains and nonsense jingles itself proves the value of repetition, besides being an assertion of the singer's musical rights. And in practice these repetitions, ridiculous as they may appear on paper, are entirely justifiable. When Purcell repeats the word 'now' ten times on end in 'Nymphs and Shepherds' no one, either singer or listener, feels the smallest compunction. It is simply a delightful vocable and is accepted as such.

Purcell's use of formal methods, whether in his simplest strophic songs, his dance-measures, or in technical devices such as the ground-bass, is rarely founded on the principles of symmetry which appealed to the 18th century. If we take his favourite triple time measure, as exemplified by the song 'Fairest Isle' or 'Come if you Dare,' with its main accents shifting from the first to the second beat of the bar, we find the element of that irregularity which Purcell loved. Doubtless this particular measure was not his invention. Other contemporary composers used it, though none with the freedom and aptness of Purcell. It is a rhythm which seems peculiarly suited to the changing stresses of English poetry, and is at least as old as the Agincourt Song.

Our King went forth to Nor - man dy with

grace and might of __ chiv - al - ry

It is not quite an effect of syncopation in the accepted sense, for the bar lines are merely conventional and do not carry any marked accentual significance. Purcell uses this measure very frequently not merely in his songs but also in his anthems where his barring in triple-time is frequently irregular, bars of six alternating with bars of three units. The implications of the barline, which were only gradually coming into existence during the seventeenth century, under the influence of the dance forms, were not so terrifying to Purcell as they would seem to have been to Lawes. Purcell treated the bar with much freedom and was not at all fettered by the implied accent.

His preference for irregular patterns and free phrasing is everywhere apparent, in the slow movements of his instrumental overtures which often consist of an uneven number of bars and rarely of multiples of four, as in his songs. Even when they consist of groups of four or eight bars, the phrases are very often un-symmetrically arranged. Thus, in the first strain of the song

'Come unto these Yellow Sands,' the whole charm
of the four-bar rhythm lies in the fact that the
phrase falls into two sections of three bars and one
bar respectively, instead of being evenly divided.
But Purcell's most characteristic measures consist of multiples of five rather than four bars. And
within this scheme the groupings are far from
regular. He will divide a group of ten bars into
six and four, and one of fifteen bars, as in the
song 'Cease O my sad soul,' into seven, five and
three. His characteristic ground basses are in
many instances (such as the grounds in the great
Lament at the end of 'Dido and Aeneas,' the
'Evening Hymn' or the noble Chaconne in G
minor) built on phrase-lengths of five bars and
the superior parts by no means always coincide
with these divisions. In his dance-measures, it is
the triple-time hornpipe with its endless subtleties of rhythm, changing accent, and irregularity
of design, that he most constantly favoured.
Well might Dr. Burney, from the standpoint of
the 18th century, regard such practices as
Gothic. Had he been living to-day he would
probably have used the word Baroque, equally
loosely and with an equal sense of disparagement.

These traits, which we may claim as the most
characteristically English part of him, do not
imply that he was indifferent to form or structure,
but rather that his feeling for design was less rigid

and conventional than that of many later composers. We are perhaps too ready to think of
form in terms of the classical ideals of balance and
symmetry. Purcell, as we shall see, tended in
later life, under the influence of the Italian example, to develop a more evenly balanced style.
He arrived at a moment in musical history when
the vocal and instrumental forms had not yet
crystallised into set moulds and when the principles of balance and contrast were much less
sharply defined than they were to become in the
next century. The tedious formalities of the
aria da capo had hardly begun to enter into
his musical economy in the last year or two
of his life. The sonata, as he knew it, was a
sequence of four movements, in which the devices
of development, which were to produce so many
sublime, as also so many 'tautological,' pages,
were scarcely understood. He was singularly free
from obsessions as to correct formal procedure.
The result was that he was able to produce music
which can be viewed as one piece, and which
often defies formal analysis. That he was capable
of writing music which was completely self-sub-
sistent and in the best sense formal, is proved by
his early Fantazias, chamber-music of the most pure
and perfect kind. In these works he shows himself
the true heir of the English instrumental school.

The Fantasy was the most characteristic and

widely practised form that had ever appeared in English chamber-music, a form in which it was generally admitted that the English composers were pre-eminent. It survived in England long after the decay of the madrigal and long after the new harmonic style had elsewhere begun to replace the old polyphonic technique. It is interesting, in view of the assumption that Purcell grew up entirely under French and Italian influences, to observe that at the outset of his career, when he was scarcely twenty-one, his first venture into purely instrumental music should have taken the form of these very traditional works. The immediate contact with the older school came, no doubt, through the influence of Locke. That Purcell mapped out for himself a course of composition on an ambitious scale seems certain from the provision he made in his manuscript for many more fantasies, arranged according to the number of parts, than he actually completed. It is tempting to speculate as to what impelled him to abandon his plan—lack of appreciation (the works were never published in his lifetime), the growing claims of his public duties, the King's well-known hatred of 'fancies,' or mere English dislike of anything too formal and schematic. It has been noticed that in his sonatas for violins published three years later, he began on a systematic plan of key-sequence and in a similar volume published after his death, the scheme is carried a stage further but never completed—the time was not ripe for a 'Well-tempered' catalogue of keys, owing to the system of tuning then in existence, nor perhaps, even if it had been, was Purcell the type of man to carry it through. He had little of Bach's Teutonic gift for driving his art to a logical conclusion or rounding it off with a moral flourish. His first extensive work for the stage was a complete opera. But he never wrote another. He did the things that came to his hand and did them with his might. But it was apparently no part of his economy to produce works that were not needed.

In the Fantasies (or Fantazias, as he called them, with his inveterate fondness for putting up a pseudo-Italian façade) he makes his nearest approach to writing completely disinterested music.[1] In style they conform to Morley's classical description of this kind of music – 'A musician taketh a point at his pleasure and

---

[1] The late Mr. Peter Warlock, in his edition of the Fantazias (Curwen, 1927) assumes that they were 'originally written for viols.' This, however, seems improbable. I am indebted to Mr. M. A. Pallis for the suggestion that they were most likely written for a complete range of violins, including the true tenor, an instrument which has unaccountably gone out of use. Purcell, in the score of 'Dioclesian,' writes specifically for 'tener violins.' The famous 'One-Note' Fantasy is, no doubt, intended to embrace a complete quintet of two violins, viola (alto), tenor and violoncello. In his edition of Playford's 'Introduction' Purcell makes the following comment on four part writing: 'In Church Musick, the Four Parts consist generally of Treble, Contra-Tenor [i.e. alto], Tenor and Bass; in Instrumental Musick commonly two Trebles, Tenor and Bass.'

wresteth and turneth it as he list, making either much or little of it according as shall seeme best in his own conceit. In this may more art be showne than in any other musicke, because the composer is tide to nothing else but that he may add, diminish and alter at his own pleasure ' – though Thomas Morley would probably have been a little shocked at some of Purcell's modulations, 'which in fantasie may never bee suffered.' Yet these works, miniatures in size but rich in their musical content, are far from being formless. An alternation of slow and quick sections, but without breaks other than a cadence, contrast of mood between the strictly contrapuntal sections and short passages of a more homophonic nature, perhaps a few bars of coda to end, sometimes incorporating hints of the previous matter, all is freely conceived and yet perfectly finished. No two of them are identical in shape but none of them are shapeless. They crowd into their brief life an experience that would take many classical composers a whole quartet on a four movement plan to equal. No chamber-music more lovely has been written than the little four-part fantasy in C minor with its haunting close which has a pathos that Wagner, with the whole apparatus of the orchestra, scarcely excelled.[1]

[1] And which, indeed, bears some striking affinities with a passage at the close of the prelude Act 3 of 'The Mastersingers.'

The five-part 'Fantasy upon one Note' is a tour de force in the old style of the 'In Nomine,' in which a phrase of long notes (here reduced to a single repeated note, middle C) is held by one instrument (the tenor) while the remaining four weave around it ingenious counterpoints. Purcell always showed an extreme partiality for such technical riddles. What is more to the point he invariably managed to write without the smallest suggestion of being under any constraint by them.

It is in the Fantasies that Purcell makes his most unmistakable acknowledgments to the English musical tradition. Whatever he might profess in the case of the violin sonatas, which were published three years later, his models for these works were not far to seek. The sonatas were ostensibly in a more modern idiom. They were written for two violins, viola da gamba and harpsichord (or organ), but when allowance is made for this fact, it must be confessed that they exhibit not a few traces of the old contrapuntal technique. Their most constant feature is a fugal movement called Canzona, which it may be noticed was also a characteristic of the sonatas that William Young had published thirty years previously. They abound in imitative passages and though the subjects are, in many cases, bolder and more extended than those of the Fantasies, there is little attempt to display the upper instruments at the expense of the lower. The sonatas are on a larger scale than the Fantasies and one, the sixth sonata of the second set, is the most ambitious single movement in all Purcell's chamber-music, being in the nature of a lengthy Chaconne. Purcell showed a singular regard for this form, which he handled with so much mastery, and later on frequently used in his dramatic works. For the rest, the structure of the sonatas is scarcely less free than that of the Fantasies. The number of movements may be anything from four to seven, labelled in Italian with all the pride of one familiar with the best precedents.[1] Their disposition varies, but the first is usually a slow movement and the last a lively one, though this is sometimes followed by a few bars of coda marked 'Adagio.' In between, there are the fugal Canzonas and triple-time Largos, which almost invariably occur, in conjunction with other short sections according to the composer's fancy. Indeed, what gives these sonatas their chief appeal is precisely that they are not cut to any fixed pattern but have each an individuality. They have features in common, but always there is the little unexpected turn that saves them from being merely repetitive. The

[1] But the explanation of these 'few terms of Art perhaps unusual' to the 'English Practitioner,' which Purcell gives in his preface, is a little naïve. Thus, 'Presto Largo, Poco Largo, or Largo by itself, *a middle movement.*'

fine dramatic opening of the Sonata in D minor (No. 3 of the first set) with the subtly marked rhythm of the Canzona which follows, the extraordinarily technical ingenuity of the Sonata in C major (No. 6) the expressive opening of the Sonata in E minor (No. 7) as grave as a lament by Dowland, the sunny atmosphere of the G major (No. 8) – one could go through the whole series with rarely a dull moment. Purcell's music may, indeed, sometimes lack mystery, but it is rarely deficient in surprise, even when he seems to trade overmuch on his own formulae. One little figure, the nearest approach to a 'finger-print' in his works, occurs so frequently in the Canzonas that it must be noted. It consists of three repeated quavers, the first coming after the beat.

This may be found all over his works.[1] The

[1] Compare, for example, the overture to the St. Cecilia's Day Ode (1692) which Handel borrowed and incorporated in his 'Water Music.'

three-note figure is also prominent, in a different form, in his Largo movements, many of which open in some such manner as this:

Purcell's music, however, is apt to defy generalisation. There is no rule in his music that cannot be reduced to naught by the importance of the exceptions. For instance, it was pointed out above that his use of the minor mode carried no hard-and-fast emotional significance. This is in the main true. Some of his happiest tunes, such as the hornpipes and the pastoral melodies, are in the minor. But in his first set of sonatas, he does seem to have started out to explore the emotional and colouristic possibilities of the various keys; the keys are arranged in sequence, each minor key being followed by its relative major, and, speaking broadly, one cannot fail to notice the more serious tone of the sonatas governed by minor-key signatures. G minor is the most ambiguous of his keys; he uses it constantly and in both senses, for hornpipes and laments. But the sonatas in D minor, A minor, E minor and C minor are all of a graver type than those in B flat, F, C, G, and D. In the second set these contrasts are less marked and there is a greater variety of modulation within the main key scheme. One sonata (No. 9 in F major) has become famous as the 'Golden Sonata' – it is the only one of Purcell's chamber-works that has endured; even the lovely and unique sonata for solo violin, a finer work in every way, has been eclipsed by this single representative of his chamber-style. It is not difficult to see why this work has survived at the expense of many others which are intrinsically better music. It is on a bigger scale than most of the other sonatas and it is much the most superficially effective work, from the players' angle, of any in the series. Its best movement is the beautiful elegiac Adagio. For the rest, its strenuous commonplaces, its grateful-ness, and its obvious desire to create an impression, are enough to account for its public favour. But players should turn rather to the sonatas in D minor, F, A minor and G in the first set and those in E flat, G minor (the Chaconne) and C major in the second set. Those who, as Purcell says in his foreword to the first set, 'carry Musical Souls about them,' will not fail to find in these lovely, inventive works many passages of supreme beauty.

It has been charged against Purcell that in his

violin sonatas he shows no particular evidence of having understood the instrument for which he wrote. Violin technique in England was no doubt somewhat backward. We have seen that the foreign virtuosi who visited this country in the later years of the Commonwealth and in the early years of the Restoration, astonished English audiences. English audiences have always been ready to be astonished by foreign virtuosi and English composers have shown little faculty for the astonishing – Purcell in his vocal works was a notable exception. But the idea that Purcell did not understand the violin is surely a little mythical. He understood it as well as contemporary experience could permit. It was a relatively new instrument as a medium for chamber-music, though it had a respectable history among 'common fiddlers.' If Purcell did not understand the violin, it is rather puzzling to account for his appointment, at the early age of eighteen, as Composer for the Violins, in succession to his master, Matthew Locke. The sonatas were written some six years later, when Purcell had already had considerable practice in writing instrumental anthems for the Chapel Royal as well as Royal odes and incidental music for stage plays. Moreover, his father had been a member of the King's private band and his uncle, who educated him, was the leader of the four and twenty violins. In these circumstances it would be surprising if Purcell did not learn to play the violin. Pelham Humfrey's opinion of Grabu, that he could not play an instrument 'and so cannot compose,' would have seemed much more like common sense in the 17th century than it may appear in these days.

On the other hand, it is true that in the sonatas Purcell does not adventure into any high flights, though he must have been familiar with the methods of Matteis. But if we regard these works, as indeed we must, as trios with continuo (organ or harpsichord) there is no particular reason for regretting that Purcell did not adopt a more brilliantly violinistic style, any more than we should complain that the Fantasies do not give the individual players more opportunity to shine. The presence of the harpsichord does not alter the fact that the sonatas are founded on a contrapuntal style. They are true chamber-music of parts and not virtuoso pieces. In the second set Purcell does indeed show some signs of developing a more showy technique, and not always to the advantage of the music. These later sonatas – how much later we do not know[1] – show a certain development in style. The Canzonas are more elaborately wrought, the closes are more varied,

---

[1] They were published posthumously by Purcell's widow and are stated to have 'already found many friends.'

and there is a stronger feeling for climax. This last was the most notable advance that Purcell made in his instrumental music and may be traced in his dramatic overtures on the Lully model. It points to a growing sense of formal construction. In his earlier works, for instance the introductory symphonies of the Chapel Royal anthems, there sometimes seems no reason why the music should come to an end just where it does. Short as the movements are there is not that sense of progression towards a premeditated close that later enabled Purcell to write fairly extended movements in one continuous piece, irregular in shape but perfectly poised and balanced in expression.

Nothing has so much hindered the possibilities of Purcell criticism as the erroneous dates that have in the past been assigned to many of his more important compositions. Faced with the baffling appearance of works which though attributed to the early stages of his career bore all the marks of a mature style, his critics have taken the simple course of saying that Purcell's art shows from start to finish no signs of development, when they have not, like Rimbault, attempted to trace its progress in the light of such assumptions as that 'Dido and Aeneas' was written by a boy of seventeen. That Purcell, alone of all the great composers, should have sprung into the world fully armed might have been put down at once as an improbable thesis. Even now that the dates of his dramatic works have been fixed with some measure of certainty, the task of criticism is not made lighter by the bewildering inconsistencies of some aspects of his work or by the equally deceptive consistency of others. The problem, in the case of his instrumental music, is complicated by the frequency with which the same forms are used, so as to lend a superficial similarity to his work at all periods, and in the case of his vocal music by the recurrence throughout his life of the same devices and methods. There are things at almost all stages of his career, both the good and the bad, which we can even now contemplate only with amazement. If the dates were not apparently unchallengeable we should find it hard to believe that certain of the Fantasies were written by a young man of twenty-one. With such beginnings in mind, it is manifestly easier to speak of change rather than development. On the whole, then, it is through a study of the vocal music that we shall best appreciate the growth of Purcell's art. For, as Henry Playford wrote in the introduction to his collection of Purcell's songs – 'His extraordinary talent in all sorts of Musick is sufficiently known, but he was especially admired for the vocal, having a peculiar genius to express the Energy of English words whereby he moved the Passions in all his Auditors.'

Chapter II

POETIC MATERIALS

PURCELL'S musical life was passed under the triple dominion of the court, the church and the stage. For the first he wrote Odes and Welcome Songs, for the second services and anthems and for the last incidental music and semi-operas. He served under three reigns – Charles II, James II and William and Mary – and during his life there were three poets-laureate – Dryden, Shadwell and Tate – of whom only one was a poet and even he not all the time. Dryden was certainly one of the most energetic writers who have ever used the English language. If there was a moment in English musical history when the union of poetry and music seemed destined to produce something in the nature of a national music-drama, it was when Dryden invited Purcell to collaborate with him in his operatic play 'King Arthur.' The foremost English poet and the leading English composer of the day – it was a promising combination.[1] The subject was

[1] 'Music,' said Purcell, 'is the exaltation of poetry. Both of them may exist apart, but they are most excellent when they are joined.'

epic. The poet was prepared to make conces-
sions to the composer and the composer was eminently well-equipped to do justice to the poet. In
point of fact, the experiment was a success but it
was never repeated. The brightest moment in
the cloudy annals of English opera was allowed
to pass without its implications being realised.
Dryden perhaps lacked, in spite of his theorising,
the steadiness of purpose which might have enabled him to see through the task of founding a
genuinely English opera and Purcell was always
willing to take up whatever lay readiest to his
hand.

Shadwell was not the man to succeed where
Dryden failed. His purely dramatic sense was in
some respects greater than that of his famous
rival, who wrote savagely of him:

> Shadwell alone, of all my sons is he
> Who stands confirmed in full stupidity.
> The rest to some faint meaning make pretence
> But Shadwell never deviates into sense.

It was grossly unfair: Shadwell frequently de-
viated into sense. True, Lord Rochester said of
him 'If Shadwell had burnt all he wrote and
printed all he spoke, he would have had more
wit and humour than any other poet.' His plays
were, nevertheless, frequently revived, and his
adaptations of Shakespeare, barbarous as they
may seem to us, kept the stage for more than a

century. As a poet he merits Dryden's adjective.[1]
But if Shadwell was dull Tate was deadly. Yet it
was the son of 'Faithful Teate' who was to collaborate with Purcell in his single perfect opera, and
the part-author of the 'new and modish' metrical
Psalms who was to share a less dubious immor-
tality by writing the libretto of 'Dido and
Aeneas.'

At the same time, it is unnecessary to take too
harsh a view of the poets with whom Purcell collaborated. In the printed page their work frequently appears deplorable, but much of it was
written with a special object in view and at its
best it is, for the given purpose, a serviceable instrument. The average level of the lyric poetry
of the age was certainly not as high as that of the
first half of the century. The songs of Herrick,
Lovelace, Suckling, Waller and Carew were of an
altogether finer stamp than those of the minor
poets and versifiers of Purcell's day. The strange
thing is that with the casual exception of his few
incidental songs in the 'Tempest,' Purcell seems
practically never to have stepped outside the con-
fines of his own period in his secular music, but
to have succumbed completely to the conventions
of his time. Stacks of verse were written about
shepherds and shepherdesses, in which lovers

[1] 'The midwife laid her hand on his thick skull,
With this prophetic blessing – "Be thou DULL." '
– Dryden, 'Absalom and Achitophel.'

sighed over the wounds delivered to them by some
cruel fair one. Every age has its conventions but
this particular convention was driven to preposterous lengths. Tags out of Shakespeare (such as
'If music be the food of love,' which a certain
Colonel Heveningham grafted on a poem that so
pleased Purcell as to draw no less than three settings from him) and weak echoes of the phraseology of the earlier Caroline poets, were turned to
the purposes of this ceaseless sighing about the
pains and penalties of unrequited passion. But
one quality most of the erotic verse of the period
undoubtedly possesses. It is eminently singable,
and if one regards the sound rather than the
sense, it is by no means unbearable. The versifiers do indeed seem to have studied to produce
words for music and to have striven to find
feminine rhymes and varied metres in the interest
of musical setting. Several of them, such as
Tom D'Urfey, whose collection 'Wit and Mirth or
Pills to Purge Melancholy' is a storehouse of
Restoration lyrics, were amateur musicians.
D'Urfey's 'On the brow of Richmond Hill,' which
Purcell set, is a fair specimen of the less conventional type of verse:

> On the brow of Richmond Hill
> Which Europe scarce can parallel,
> Ev'ry eye such wonders fill
>   To view the prospect round;

Where the silver Thames doth glide
And stately courts are edified,
Meadows deck'd in summer's pride
  With verdant beauties crown'd;

Lovely Cynthia passing by,
With brighter glories blest my eye.
Ah, then in vain, in vain, said I,
  The fields and flowers do shine;
Nature in this charming place,
Created pleasures in excess,
But all are poor to Cynthia's face,
  Whose features are divine.

As poetry it does not amount to much and the flat
line at the end cripples it as a song. But it has
movement and is shapely. Moreover it sings.
Dryden himself was often far less happy, and his
consciousness of being 'cramped' by music led him
into tedious inversions such as:

Shepherd, Shepherd, leave decoying,
Pipes are sweet a summer's day,
Let us music be enjoying
Thus to beauty tribute pay.

Here with leaves and flowers entwining
Trip we nimbly o'er the ground.
For the past have no repining,
Play and dance a merry round.

Which, apart from one good line, reads very
much as though it were a translation made for
music. The general tone of the lyrical verse in
Purcell's operas is no higher than this and frequently very much below it. On the other hand,

in some of the dialogues and humorous scenes, the language is often entirely devoid of artificiality. Some of Purcell's raciest work is in a vein of natural colloquial speech. He developed this colloquial faculty in the numerous rounds and catches which he set, and which, though in many instances marred by the impropriety of the words, were a valuable contributory influence on his style. Catches and rounds were a traditional feature of English music. There is perhaps no form which has had so long and continuous a history from the days of the famous 'Sumer is icumen in' (incidentally on a ground bass) to the early 19th century. Purcell wrote scores of such things.

In order to see Purcell under the severest handicap to his text, we must turn to the ceremonial Odes and Welcome Songs which he wrote with unfailing diligence once or twice every year from 1680 to the date of his death. They were frankly occasional pieces and probably never had more than a single performance. Some member of the royal family has a birthday and Purcell writes an Ode on some doggerel verses by the poet-laureate. Or the king returns from Newmarket and London goes into dutiful ecstasies. Again, Purcell obliges with an ode. Our feeling of the falsity of these expressions may tempt us into regarding Purcell's music as the product of mere official routine.

This is not altogether the case. The crown was popular. Such incidents as the Rye House Plot stirred national feeling. The king's return to London rarely failed to be celebrated with 'publick demonstrations of Joy, as ringing of bells, store of bonfires, etc.' Purcell was quite able in such circumstances to rise to the occasion without putting his tongue in his cheek. But his poets were not so happy. They were usually merely grotesque. Thus the appropriately named Thomas Flatman can write:

> From these serene and rapturous joys
>   A country life alone can give,
> Exempt from tumult and from noise,
> Where Kings forget the troubles of their reigns,
> And are almost as happy as their humble swains,
>   By feeling that they live,
> Behold th' indulgent Prince is come
> To view the Conquests of His mercy shown
> To the new Proselytes of His mighty Town
> And men and Angels bid him welcome Home.

Purcell can make nothing of these verses. But the pastoral suggestion enables him to write a charming instrumental interlude and he can place his violins high up in thirds, like flutes. When he comes to the appalling words

> With trumpets and shouts we receive the World's wonder
> And let the clouds echo His welcome with thunder

he can at least give the voice a trumpet figure (echoed by the instruments) and place it in the significant key of D major. For the rest he is dependent on the chance of seizing on a natural image as in 'Swifter, Isis, flow' or, more daringly, at the words 'Tune all your strings' he can make the violins sound their open notes in rapid reiteration as if tuning up (in 'Ye Tuneful Muses'). Faced with the words 'From the rattling of drums' he writes a whole passage on a tonic and dominant bass, the drum-tunings, and 'To music's softer but yet kind and pleasing melody' he can add the ingratiating accompaniment of two flutes. Or if he has the words, 'Be lively then and gay' he can introduce into his bass the popular dance tune of the day 'Hey boys, up go we,' while 'Sound the trumpet, beat the drum' is an obvious opening for a combination of trumpet calls and drum-notes, rendered by the strings. Nothing is more charming in all Purcell's music than the way he suggests one instrument on another, by transferring, as it were metaphorically, the characteristic procedure of the one to the other.

It must not be inferred, however, that Purcell's music in these Royal odes amounts to no more than a desperate snatching at musical images. Purcell was very much dependent on his words, but he was not their slave. Indeed it is the very flatness of the words in many cases that forces him to ignore them and build up a movement on purely musical lines. One of the finest of his odes

'Why are all the Muses mute?' was based on a dull poem in which James II is absurdly hailed as Caesar and his virtues enshrined in euphemistic phraseology. Whether it was James or whether Caesar that inspired Purcell does not much matter, but the fact is that not even Bach wrote a more heart-easing melody than that to which Purcell set the words 'Caesar for milder virtues honoured more.' It descends into E flat immediately after a cadence in G minor. There is a Brahmsian tenderness about it which seems to have no place in the scheme of things. We can only wonder how it got there. Purcell was capable of these surprising intrusions which carry him right outside his period and give his music an extraordinary prophetic quality.

Purcell's odes for Queen Mary seem to have been touched with a more personal sentiment. The 'gentle Queen'[1] was universally beloved, and when she died Purcell wrote one of the very

---

[1] William is reported to have said of her – 'She had no fault – none; you knew her well, but you could not know – nobody but myself could know – her goodness.' It was Queen Mary who set the fashion of making fringes or Knotting. 'She was soon imitated, not only by her maids of honour, but by all the ladies of distinction throughout the Kingdom, and so fashionable was the labour, of a sudden, grown that not only assembly rooms and visiting rooms, but the streets, the roads, nay the very playhouses were witness of their pretty industry; it was considered a wonder that the Churches escaped.' (Miss Strickland's 'Queens of England.') Purcell deals humorously with this fashion in 'The Knotting Song' (words by Sir Charles Sedley) in which the musical phrases twine in and out so amusingly.

greatest of his elegies, which though it has the practical drawback of being couched in Latin, must remain as one of the most moving things he ever wrote – Bach never achieved a more intimate expression of tender pathos. Purcell was stirred by the subject of Death as by no other emotion – the loss of three of his children in infancy and the possible recognition that he himself suffered from an inherited disease (which was to bring about his early death in his thirty-seventh year) were enough to keep the subject ever before him. His expressions of joy, on the occasions of his ceremonial pieces, are apt here and there to have an air of forced cheerfulness or at least of resort to a stereotyped formula, but his laments, whether for his friend Locke or the well-liked publisher Playford,[1] invariably ring true. Queen Mary, unlike her consort, seems to have had more than a passing fancy for music, though Hawkins' story of her preference for the ballad 'Cold and Raw,' which Purcell as a joke introduced into his Birthday Ode 'Love's Goddess sure' in 1692, seems to indicate that her tastes were a little simple. At any rate it was for her rather than the 'renown'd Nassau' that Purcell wrote his yearly odes during the last six years of his life. The ode for 1689 was

[1] Dr. Cummings thought that the 'Elegy on the death of John Playford' (Nahum Tate) referred to John Playford Junior, a nephew of the publisher, but Mr. Frank Kidson in 'Grove' assigns it to the elder Playford.

written by Shadwell. It was a poor effort. What could Purcell do with such lines as:

> Now does the glorious day appear,
> The mightiest day of all the year ;
> Not any one such Joy could bring.
> Not that which ushers in the spring.

D'Urfey's ode 'Arise my muse' in the following year was a little less flat:

> Arise, my muse, and to the tuneful lyre
>   Compose a mighty Ode
> Whose charming Nature may Inspire
>   The Bosom of some listening god
> To consecrate thy bold Adventurous Verse
> And Gloriana's Fame Disperse
> O'er the wide confines of the Universe.

This was the type of 'bold, adventurous verse' that Purcell had constantly to set. But he makes the best of his task and there is no indication that he found it totally uncongenial. These royal odes contain some splendid pages. In form they are merely a secular version of his Chapel Royal anthems with the 'verse' solos and duets, instrumental ritornelli, and interspersed choruses of his earlier church style. As in the church anthems, we can see him schooling himself in dramatic expression. Whenever the words give him a chance, he seizes on them for a purely musical expression, repeating them without shame. He dwells on such words as 'sound' and 'ring.' All the forms which he afterwards used so effectively in his dramatic works are present here in embryo – the solos on a ground bass (e.g. 'See the glittering Ruler of the Day' in the 1690 Ode, with its changing rhythmic accents), the delicious symphonies and ritornelli, and the bold and massive choruses. How much delightful music lies locked up in these occasional Odes ! How to rescue it from the dead weight of this heavy-handed verse ? The florid writing on such words as 'mighty,' 'arise,' 'glory' and the like are pure Purcell. The modulatory freedom, the balance and contrast of keys, are purely his. Repetitions of the comprehensive words 'all,' 'no,' 'on' and the like are equally characteristic:

> But glory cryes go on,
> On, on, illustrious man;
> Leave not the work undone
> Thou hast so well begun:
> Go on, great Prince, go on.

And by the time Purcell has finished, the illustrious subject of the panegyric has moved on and on and on, through several pages.

Three works, of more enduring significance, stand apart from the bulk of these occasional pieces and topical effusions – the 'Yorkshire Feast Song,' the Ode for St. Cecilia's Day (1692) and the 'Te Deum and Jubilate' also written for the Cecilian celebration, in 1694.[1] The Yorkshire

[1] 'The 22nd November, being St. Cecilia's Day, is observed through all Europe by the lovers of Music. On that Day, or the

Feast was an annual rally of the county gentry in London. The fact that music played an important part in its programme rather dispels the idea that musical culture was not fairly widespread in the later 17th century. We can scarcely imagine the promoters of a city dinner requisitioning, in these days, a new work by Elgar. It was the kind of thing that Purcell did supremely well. There has never been a composer in history who could rise to the occasion with such perfect ease and with such complete lack of self-consciousness as he did. The words were by Tom D'Urfey and D'Urfey set out to excel himself. York, after the usual pseudo-classical convention of the time, is hailed as Brigantium ('honoured with a race divine') and the 'Bashful Thames' is rather ashamed of the comparative insignificance of London. As an example of local patriotism it is superb. And Purcell's music is stirring, festive, exciting. He writes a fanfare-like overture, declamatory recitatives in which words like 'martial'

next when it falls on a Sunday, most of the lovers of Music, whereof many are persons of the first rank, meet at Stationers' Hall in London, not through a principle of superstition but to propagate the advancement of that divine science. A splendid entertainment is provided and before it always a performance of Music by the best voices and hands in town: the words which are always in the patroness's praise, are set by some of the greatest Masters in Town. . . . The feast is one of the genteelest in the world; there are no formalities nor gatherings like at others, and the appearance there is always very splendid. While the company is at table the Hautbois and Trumpets play successively.' ('Gentleman's Journal' 1692.)

and 'towering' are finely painted in florid passages, and the lovely tenor solo with two recorders
(flutes) dealing with the 'Bashful Thames.' The
solos, such as 'The Pale and purple Rose'[1] and
the beautiful song on a ground bass 'So when the
glittering Queen of Night,' are among Purcell's
best efforts. It can be imagined how the closing
recitative with its thrilling choral interjections and
the final outburst of 'Long flourish the city and
county of York' must have stirred the assembly to
a pitch of enthusiasm. It is a magnificent occasional piece. Moreover, except in one particular
which we shall notice later on in connection with
the anthems, it is still quite practicable.

The Cecilian celebrations seem to have been
inaugurated in the year 1683. Purcell wrote three
odes and it is rather astonishing that at the age of
twenty-four when there were such masters as
Blow in the field, his genius should have been so
early recognised. The event was promoted by an
organisation known as the Musical Society, to
which Purcell professes himself under an obligation in the preface to his first published ode. These
early Cecilian odes are unfortunately put out of

---

[1] Dr. Burney has a pleasant fancy about this song. 'An
ingenious but comic idea that seems to mark Purcell's resources,
in whatever he wished to express by picturesque music, is the
military cast he has given to the base of this song . . . which
though the air itself is no more than a common languid minuet,
reminds us perpetually of the drums, skirmishes, and battles,
of the contending houses of York and Lancaster.'

court by the wretched banality of the words. Their only importance lies in Purcell's treatment of the instrumental accompaniments. The form is again derived from that of the Chapel Royal anthem, with its 'verses' for alto, tenor and bass, its full choruses and instrumental ritornelli. We can see anticipations of his later dramatic style in his settings of individual words (such as 'troubled,' on a downward portamento) and in his use of descending chromatic chords. These works may be totally dead from a practical standpoint, but we cannot ignore them, as contributory influences on the formation of his dramatic style.

The 1692 Ode 'Hail, bright Cecilia' is in a different category. Dr. Nicholas Brady's poem is, indeed, conventional enough, but it is peculiarly rich in the kind of images that Purcell loved, not merely those relating directly to his art, but images of motion, effects of antithesis, and words that lend themselves to his favourite devices of repetition, antiphony and metaphorical illustration. The great invocation to Music is one of Purcell's most memorable passages:

> Soul of the World, inspired by thee
> The jarring seeds of matter did agree.
> Thou didst the scattered atoms bind
> Which by thy laws of true proportion joined
> Made up of various parts one perfect harmony.

It is quite short, a mere forty-three bars, but it has

an extraordinary spaciousness. The chief solos in the work are for male alto and at the first performance they seem to have been taken by Purcell himself. The whole scheme of the work is finely planned, as well in the balance and contrast of its keys, which are much more adventurous than those of Handel's better known Ode of 1739, as in the lay-out of the solo and ensemble numbers, and the instrumentation, which includes flutes, oboes, trumpets, strings and drums, with harpsichord and organ.[1] Purcell anticipates Handel's use of obbligato instruments for the various sections in which they are mentioned – the 'airy violin,' the 'am'rous flute,' the 'fife and all the harmony of War.' For the overture he adopts his five-movement sonata plan, passing through the principal keys he proposes to employ later, and then after a short bass solo, comes the thrilling cry from the full chorus, 'Hail ! bright Cecilia,' with the invocatory word placed strikingly on the off-beat so as to give greater immediacy to the attack on the fugal entry that follows. This one blank beat, a momentary silence between the solo and the chorus, is a master-stroke of dramatic effect. Purcell's rests, here and in the concluding bars of the 'Soul of the World' chorus, are as eloquent as his notes. The

[1] The flutes and oboes do not play together, as apparently these instruments were doubled by the same player in Purcell's day. (Dr. E. J. Dent, 'Foundations of English Opera.')

ascending notes of the invocation are resumed in the final chorus but in immense augmentation and in D major instead of minor. It is not an easy work. All the voices are employed in extremely florid passages. Purcell's vocal demands increased enormously in his later works and only a highly trained choir could do this music justice. The fantastic alto solo ' 'Tis Nature's Voice' pushes decorative word-painting to the farthest point of virtuosity, though probably it looks more fearsome on paper than it actually is. Few of Purcell's works show a greater consistency of style than this splendid Ode.

The 'Te Deum and Jubilate' written for the celebration in 1694 is on an even more lavish scale. There are perhaps greater inequalities in it than in the Cecilian Ode and for modern tastes some of the descriptive writing may seem overdone, but it was a work written for a special festive occasion and much dependent on brilliant execution. Its curious history has often been told. It was given yearly at the Three Choirs' Festivals from the date of their inauguration until 1713 when it was alternated with Handel's Utrecht Te Deum and for the next thirty years the works were performed in turn. Then Handel's Dettingen Te Deum superseded it altogether. It was to Dr. Boyce that it owed its revival and incidentally the astonishing treatment to which it was subjected.

Boyce re-scored it and introduced symphonies in between the various sections, increasing the length by more than half and generally dressing it up in Handelian frills.[1]   From this deplorable plight it was rescued by the late Sir Frederick Bridge, who however, though scrupulous in all other respects, seems to have baulked at the extremes of Purcell's florid writing and given a hint to the timid by bracketing certain passages for optional omission, and by suggesting that some of the verse-solos might be sung by the choral voices. It is a counsel of imperfection which does not really solve Purcell's special problems.

One of these, and it is a rather grave problem, applying equally to his anthems and his dramatic pieces, is the use of the alto voice in so much of Purcell's most difficult music. Purcell has had, in the course of time, almost every conceivable kind of bad luck, serving to hinder the performance of his music and the growth of a practical tradition. But this misfortune has lain more heavily upon him than any other. Had he been himself a tenor instead of an alto, we might not have had quite so much of his work pitched in this particular register, though there is no doubt that the male alto,

[1] Boyce has been much, and rightly, castigated for this wanton example of the worst type of editing. But a very similar procedure has been adopted in a modern edition of 'Mad Bess,' a song which depends for its entire effect on the sudden contrasts of mood between the various sections. The introduction of pianoforte interludes completely destroys Purcell's idea.

besides being inevitable in cathedral music and particularly in the verse-anthems of the time, was a very popular solo voice in Purcell's day. Nowadays it is scarcely cultivated outside the sphere of male voice choirs, if we except the type of falsetto which usually does duty for it in church. 'Feigned voices,' as Matthew Locke tells us, were not unknown in Purcell's day. Yet the male alto (or counter-tenor) is a real voice and a traditionally English one. Apart from the fact that in colour and texture it differs from the contralto, it has, or should have, a compass that is at once higher than the tenor and lower than the female alto voice, so that for contraltos much of Purcell's music lies in an awkward tessitura besides requiring an agility which few contraltos possess. But the problem ought to be faced and not evaded. Alto voices are not incapable of development. The difficulty is one which is met with frequently in the case of the madrigals and wholesale re-arrangement or transposition will not solve it. The older composers wrote for a wide range of voices. The study of Purcell would certainly tend to do away with the vogue of the nondescript type of voice which modern English composers in their vocal music seem so often to encourage. The characteristic English voice of to-day is a mezzo-soprano or a baritone, when it is not a tenor that is a baritone forced up. Purcell wrote for real sopranos and real basses and in his inner parts used the fullest range of voice.[1] A diagrammatic analysis of some of his typical songs would probably reveal the fact that his music demands not merely a wide compass but a fairly prevalent use of the more extreme and characteristic levels of the voice.

When we turn to Purcell's church music, it is to find greater inequalities but not lesser glories than in his secular music. He was, as we have seen, schooled in the ecclesiastical tradition. The Chapel Royal was his nursery and it was governed in his youth by two men, Cooke and Humfrey, whose leanings were towards the dramatic style. Purcell seems to have written very little pure service music and those of his services which survive, especially as lugubriously performed by modern church choirs, are, at least to one pair of ears, among his tamest effusions. They are correct, orthodox, chaste and unadventurous. With the anthems it is a different story. When we lament the fact that so often his music was found in company with the verse of the miserable poetasters of his time, we are apt to overlook the fact that his earliest efforts were associated with

---

[1] English basses seem to have enjoyed in the 16th and 17th centuries a reputation for profundity as great as that of the Russian basses in our day. Purcell has been credited with the invention of the florid bass solo, another of the things, perhaps, that Handel derived from him.

the magnificent poetry of Hebrew prophets.[1] The conventions of the period led to the selection of texts, as Bumpus has pointed out in his 'Cathedral Music,' notable for their highly coloured imagery. The anthem was the most characteristic form of English church music. Pepys constantly refers to it and Hawkins tells us of a modish habit of the gentlemen of the time, who escorted a lady to the afternoon service at St. Paul's, especially if there was a new anthem. It may not have been a very religious practice but it was at least a sign of musical interest. The Chapel Royal anthems were quite frankly a musical entertainment. With

[1] Cf. 'T. Brown to his unknown friend Mr. Henry Purcell upon his Excellent Compositions in the first and second books of "Harmonia Sacra"'

> For where the Author's scanty words have fail'd,
> Your happier Graces, Purcell, have prevail'd.
> And surely none but you with equal Ease,
> Could add to *David* and make Durfy please.

Purcell edited the volume 'Harmonia Sacra' in 1688. It was dedicated to Bishop Ken. There are twenty-nine pieces, twelve by Purcell, four by Locke, three by Humfrey and seven by Blow, etc. Playford (junior) writes in the preface: 'As for the musical part, it was composed by the most Skilful Masters of the Age; and though some of them are now dead, yet their composures have been review'd by Mr. Henry Purcell, whose tender regard for the Reputation of those great Men made him careful that nothing should be published which, through the negligence of Transcribers, might reflect upon their Memory.' Part two contains Purcell's splendid scena 'In Guilty Night.' This publication, which reached a third edition in 1714, contains some of Purcell's finest sacred music, including the Morning and Evening Hymns (words by Dr. Fuller), 'Job's Curse' (words adapted by Dr. Taylor, Bishop of Down), George Herbert's 'With sick and famished eyes,' Dr. Fuller's 'Penitential Hymn' and the poem 'Upon a quiet conscience' which is attributed to Charles I.

their instrumental ritornelli, their brilliant solos, designed to show off the voice of the Rev. John Gostling, or some other famous chanter, their choruses and final alleluias, they were an extremely spectacular feature of Restoration religion. It is useless to try to reproduce these things under the decorous conditions of the modern parish church. They were not written for the parish church or even the local cathedral but for the very special circumstances of a highly sophisticated royal chapel, which employed a band of violins to give colour to the religious entertainment that was mapped out for the diversion of the royal ear. No good can be done to Purcell by pretending that he is a very feasible composer, under the ordinary conditions of church services to-day.

Dr. Arne, writing to Garrick, said that Purcell's dramatic music, though excellent enough, was too 'cathedral' in style. The criticism has more often been put the other way round, that Purcell's church music is too theatrical. Certainly there are superficial resemblances of style, but few composers ever had a finer appreciation of the dramatically appropriate, and the idea that Purcell was unable to distinguish between the Psalms of David and the texts of Dryden or D'Urfey, is too superficial to need refutation. He had, in his church music, not less than in his stage music, a keen sense

of the spirit of place, but we have to bear in mind
what the place was – the Royal Chapel or Westminster Abbey (not the parish church) and what
the occasion was – a festive service, or a coronation.
Purcell was singularly loyal to his chosen forms
and the overtures which he wrote to his anthems
are in many cases indistinguishable in appearance
from the dramatic overtures – that is, a slow movement in four-time followed by a fugal movement
in triple time. The stately processional tone of the
former is reproduced in the anthems and dramatic
works alike. The opening of the anthem 'Why do
the Heathen' is, for instance, almost identical with
the opening of the 'Dido and Aeneas' overture.
And there is no reason why it should not be.
There is a seriousness of approach common to
both. Yet the 'Dido' overture subsequently develops on much more dramatic lines. The only
inference to be drawn is that Purcell founded his
dramatic style on the methods he employed in his
church works, but as soon as that style began to
develop there is a marked divergence. Nor is
it true, as is sometimes said, that the instrumental
parts of Purcell's anthems bear no relation to the
subject in hand. On the contrary they frequently
contain thematic anticipations and résumés of the
leading vocal themes. 'O sing unto the Lord'
opens in a definitely jubilant mood while in 'Unto
Thee I will cry' the general tone of the anthem is

clearly foreshadowed by the overture. The well-known 'Bell Anthem' ('Rejoice in the Lord alway') has a characteristic descending scale passage used as a ground bass.[1] No doubt these traits were developed tentatively at first but Purcell's dramatic instinct was much too strong for him to be content with a mere abstract formula. His very choice of keys for his anthems is significant. The great coronation anthem 'My Heart is Inditing of a good matter' is dominated by the key of C major and the particularly spacious instrumental sections, treated in a rather more scholastic manner than usual seem to hint that the 'good matter' in hand could best be expressed by good counterpoint.

The general form of the anthems, apart from those written for special occasions at Westminster Abbey when additional voices would be requisitioned, is very similar throughout. After the overture, a passage for men's voices (A.T.B.) either solo or in combination, known as the 'verse,' and less often for full chorus, closing with an instrumental ritornello; then a further 'verse' passage with possibly a fairly extended solo,

[1] There is some doubt as to whether the title ('Bell Anthem') was bestowed on it by Purcell himself or another. But the effect was clearly noticed and the name is found in a contemporary MS. of the work. Dr. Ernest Walker says that Purcell, in his use of strings, 'probably never dreamt for a moment of imitating bells.' But this was precisely the kind of musical onomatopoeia that Purcell loved. Compare the anthem 'O Praise God in His holiness' where the strings have a trumpet-like flourish, and the opening bass solo in 'Awake, awake, put on thy strength.'

followed by a new ritornello; then a repetition of
the opening symphony; another 'verse' and a final
chorus with the customary alleluias. The order
may vary but the constituent parts are generally
as indicated. Actually it is the instrumental
parts that at once give unity to the work and
afford relief to the declamatory passages. They
have an artistic justification as affording an opportunity to dwell on the matter of the text. The
notion that they were inserted merely to enable
Charles II to beat time with his hand and brighten
up the service generally is a little too simple.
These works were, in fact, short cantatas and there
seems no reason for rejecting what is a fundamental part of their design. It is certain that the
tone of many of the anthems is, according to our
thinking, somewhat gay, and the choice of texts
inclining to expressions of rejoicing is apt to colour
the music in a sense that has come to be regarded
as secular. Evelyn's opinion that the introduction of symphonies was 'better suiting a
tavern, or a playhouse, than a church' is the sedate
view. Pepys, on the other hand, is frequently
enthusiastic over the anthem and Pepys was much
more a man of his time.

To modern ears the treatment of such a passage
as that beginning 'Think no scorn of me' (in the
anthem 'Unto Thee will I cry') with its numerous
repetitions of phrase and the realistic suggestion of

going 'down, down, down' into the pit (in fact to bottom D) may seem to offend against the canons of decent restraint in ecclesiastical music. But it is no different from many of the things we are accustomed to in religious oratorio, except that the declamation is more vivid. It is only the decorum of a church service that seems imperilled by these occasional declamatory excesses. We have to accept them at their face value; it is useless to try to tone them down. So, too, when Purcell writes a jolly salvationist tune at the words 'Praisèd be the Lord' there is nothing to be done except sing it lustily and at a brisk pace. The religious sentiment of many of these anthems of praise is peculiarly breezy. Nothing quite like them had appeared in English church music before or has been known since. They certainly represent the mood of the church militant and so far from their being over-expressed on the instrumental side, they occasionally seem to require the big drum, cymbals and brass of General Booth's Army to do them complete justice. The alleluias, the triple-time measures, the unabashed rhythms and swinging tunes are a good deal less offensive than the insipid sentimentalities of much Victorian church music.

But it would be a grave mistake to assume that this is the only side of Purcell's religious music. It is a characteristic side and when one considers

the nature of the Hebrew texts on which many of
his anthems are based, it is impossible to say that
his settings are inappropriate. Purcell's music
might indeed find a more congenial home in
synagogues than among congregations that have
after two centuries of conventional droning of the
'lessons' largely lost a sense of the living poetry of
the Hebrew scriptures. To Purcell all this was
new and vivid, and the poetry stirred him by its
highly coloured images in a way that he might
have been stirred by a page of Shakespeare. His
music is neither secular nor religious. It is simply
poetic, expressive, or as it ought no doubt to be
labelled to-day, expressionistic. In the brilliant,
enthusiastic work 'My beloved spake' we feel that
he has really been caught by the poetry and has
given free rein to his feeling. In 'It is a good thing
to give thanks' he rings every variety of change on
the word alleluia. It is a dull, long-winded,
repetitive anthem in some respects but it is not
ashamed of playing with the idea of praise. Sometimes he surprises us with an instrumental ritornello of Bach-like breadth and sweep, as in the
early anthem 'Behold now praise the Lord,' or
again he paints in a mood or touches a whole
scene with pictorial life, as in the section 'Sorrow
and mourning shall flee away' in the anthem
'Awake, awake, put on thy strength.' Everything
that is capable of expressive realisation in music

he seizes on. It is not by any means always an extravagant expression and the peculiar Purcell-ian intimacy and tenderness serve to give many of his pages a touching human expression. In the anthem which he wrote for the Coronation of James II, in 1685, he rises to a height unsurpassed anywhere in his church music. One can almost realise in it the very vaultings of the Cathedral nave, with which he was so intimately familiar. Its eight-part choruses are all on the most lofty scale. The unsettled tonalities of the overture all pressing forward to the statement of the main key of C major, the elaborate fugal movement which follows, the opening choruses with strings in four parts independently woven in, the contrast and division of the voices, the change of mood at the first reference to the 'queen all glorious within,' the rapid succession of keys that lead to the principal expression of jubilant rejoicing, then the resumption of the introductory symphony, a contrasting section in a graver key and finally the great choral outburst 'Praise the Lord, O Jerusalem,' a page which for its massive choral effect and bold sequence of harmonies is unequalled by any-thing in Purcell. It is in this work rather than the over-praised 'Jehova quam multi sunt hostes' which in spite of one or two splendid passages is a far less consistently fine inspiration, that Purcell touches his greatest heights in religious ceremonial music.

Purcell's anthems have suffered a harder fate than almost any other branch of his art. They have been severely criticised from the standpoint of religious sentiment. They have been wantonly maltreated by editors and they have been sung, when sung at all, in a style more appropriate to the wailings of the penitential psalms than to the lusty and exuberant emotions of joy and praise which so many of them express. Moreover the dullness of their performance, based on misconceptions of the speed at which they should be taken, has been emphasised by the choice of the duller specimens of his art and the neglect of the more vigorous examples. There are certainly greater inequalities in Purcell's church music than elsewhere, but such anthems as 'My beloved spake,' 'The Lord is my Light,' 'I will give thanks' and 'Why do the Heathen' contain much noble and expressive music, while the ceremonial anthems such as 'My heart is inditing' are worthy to rank among the finest choral works of Handel. It remains true, however, that most of these anthems demand special treatment which puts them outside the range of ordinary church use. For festive occasions and for concert performance they present a practically unexplored repertoire. In a period which is again reverting to the shorter choral forms, these works deserve study. By the side of Handel's oratorio choruses many of Purcell's must seem brief to the point of spareness, but he manages to pack an extraordinary amount of vital experience into a short space. It was not Handel, but Purcell, who brought into English music the type of broad and massive choral effect, though it is not necessary that Purcell any more than Bach (or indeed Handel himself) should be sung on the scale of the modern Handelian choir.

It is by way of Purcell's treatment of the choral episodes that we may conveniently pass to his earliest essays in theatre-music. Purcell's introduction to the stage dates from the production of Nat Lee's 'Theodosius' in 1680. He was twenty-one. It was a momentous year which saw also the production of his first welcome song, his appointment as organist of Westminster Abbey and the composition of his earliest string fantasies. Hitherto, apart from some juvenile anthems, a few single songs, and the Matthew Locke elegy, he had written little, but he had been busy perfecting his technique, copying and studying the methods of his seniors. Suddenly he emerges as a fully fledged composer. 'Theodosius' is a work of little practical importance. The music is not even especially characteristic but it contains the seeds of several of the dramatic forms which Purcell used later in his stage music. The only instruments available for the performance seem to have been a harpsichord and two recorders. For this reason the usual overture and act tunes are wanting, the latter being replaced by songs and duets of a formal nature, having no direct bearing on the action but being in the nature of a general commentary on the situation and sung between the scenes. The songs are indeed in a graceful vein and being no doubt sung in a static position, they have little dramatic significance, but 'Hail to the myrtle shade' is interesting as a prototype of the triple-time measures with their changing accents that we have noted earlier on, while another, sung after the fourth act, has a lovely flowing movement within a perfectly balanced metrical scheme that Purcell rarely attempted. It is a glorious tune, of a type and shape that do not often occur in Purcell, but quite out of keeping with the gory sentiments of the words. For the rest there is a virginal freshness about the whole score, a directness in the word setting and a completely unforced expression.

The scene which gives the play its musical importance in Purcell's development is the opening Temple scene which is the forerunner of the many scenes of ceremonial in his later works. The taste for ritualistic episodes was probably derived immediately from the librettos of Quinault and the French opera of Lully. Such episodes provided the most obvious chance for the introduction of music, with recitatives and choral movements. Purcell opens with a bass solo, 'Prepare, prepare, the rites begin,' cast in a melodious declamatory vein which shows already his instinct for dramatic invocation. The solo is echoed by a trio of voices, built on the same bass part. Purcell's sense of stage-atmosphere declares itself at once in the brief ensembles with their dramatic use of rests. The initiatory songs are unhappily marred by the rather mincing nature of the words, but there is one exquisite little movement in which Purcell makes the best use of his scanty instruments as an accompaniment to the bass solo 'Hark, behold the heavenly choir,' the flutes playing high up in thirds while the voice is kept in unison with the harpsichord bass. The music is all through touched with a naïve and unaffected simplicity. Almost all the words are set syllabically and there is practically no repetition of phrases. The same key prevails throughout except for an occasional song.

For D'Urfey's 'Sir Barnaby Whigg' in the following year Purcell wrote one song, 'Blow, Boreas, Blow,' which Burney declared to be more 'superannuated' in his day than any of Purcell's songs. It is a blustering nautical scena for tenor and bass, which probably was very amusing in the play. In tone it foreshadows many of Purcell's bravura songs, especially those for the bass voice. 'Circe' in 1685, was a notable step forward.[1] Purcell was now in the full maturity of his technical powers. Here again he is faced with a long, sacrificial scene. The play, which need not detain us, as Purcell's aid was apparently sought only in this one scene, deals somewhat freely with the Greek legend of Iphigenia in Tauris. The scene is introduced by a brief instrumental prelude leading straight into the priest's invocation (bass solo) which is then taken up by the chorus and developed at length. The measured tread of the instruments, the impressive repetitions of the words 'we must, we must' (sacrifice) divided by echoing phrases on the strings, are very similar in style to the sacrificial scene at the opening of 'King Arthur.' But the recitative is much more stolid and indeed if it is rightly attributed to Purcell, as it no doubt must be, is rather dull work for him. The choruses are more vital and are effectively repeated. Then comes a passage for two women soloists, the first part of which with its declamatory introduction, followed by a splendidly vigorous movement on a running bass, is more characteristically Purcellian. There are frequent changes of tempo, an alternation of solo passages and chorus, a dance of magicians and a

[1] The date is conjectural. The music was ascribed by Downes ('Roscius Anglicanus') to Banister but this probably referred to an earlier production. The weight of opinion is in favour of Purcell's authorship of the 'Circe' music now attributed to him.

final invocation, 'Pluto, arise,' very powerfully set for bass solo and unmistakably touched by a master-hand. This, although somewhat unsatisfactory from an operatic standpoint, concludes the music on a dramatic note and the scene ends with spoken dialogue. 'Circe' and 'Theodosius,' totally impracticable as they are to-day, are nevertheless of interest as stages in Purcell's development. 'Circe' shows a much surer grasp of the constructive values of key-contrast and restatement. The choruses are worked out at greater length and with a finer sense of climax, while the instruments are definitely absorbed into the dramatic scheme. The ritualistic element which is to recur in several of Purcell's later works is the basis of his extended choral movements. It is inevitably static in principle but it has not ceased to be theatrically effective from that day to this.

During the next few years, Purcell wrote little for the theatre except incidental songs and the only play in which he was concerned that calls for notice is D'Urfey's comedy 'A Fool's Preferment,' a version of Fletcher's 'Noble Gentleman,' which has half a dozen songs of a kind that was very popular in the 17th century. These are the so-called mad songs.[1] They are of two kinds

[1] 'The English have more songs on the subject of madness than any of their neighbours' (Bishop Percy). Feigned madness was a common form of begging in the earlier times.

– one in which the subject is represented as genuinely distracted by grief or disappointed love (such as the well-known 'Bess o' Bedlam,' Purcell's finest song in the scena form) and the other in which, for dramatic or comic purposes, the subject performs 'all the degrees of madness' – such is the 'whimsical variety' with which Altisidora teases the grotesque Knight in 'Don Quixote.'[1]

In D'Urfey's comedy the songs are sung by a character who is discovered 'crown'd with flowers and antickly drest.' They are all apparently self-contained songs instead of being welded into one continuous scena but they exhibit various degrees of melancholy madness, from the touching 'Fled is my love' and ' 'Tis Death alone,' in a declamatory style, to the lilting three-four measures of 'There's nothing so fatal as woman,' one of Purcell's most delightful colloquial songs, and the fantastically worded 'I'll sail upon the Dog-star,' which is a brilliant bravura effort. They are all for tenor voice and are eminently detachable. In a later scene there is a 'Dialogue between Jockey and Jenny,' a wooing duet of the

[1] This is the well known song 'From Rosy Bow'rs,' the 'last song that Mr. Purcell sett, it being in his sickness.' D'Urfey himself characterises the various moods as 'sullenly mad, mirthfully mad – a swift movement – melancholy madness, fantastically mad, and stark mad.' Compare also the powerful bass song 'Let the dreadful Engines' in the first part of 'Don Quixote' sung by Cardenio 'in a wild posture.'

usual suggestive Restoration type, which is described as a 'Scotch Song' on the strength of its
slight excursion into dialect. These imitation
dialect songs became very fashionable during the
reign of Charles II. There are not necessarily
any marked Scottish characteristics in the music.
This one is set in a lively six-four movement
without breaks between the lines.[1]

Such was the comparatively limited experience
of the stage with which Purcell embarked, round
about the end of his thirtieth year, on the composition of his first and only complete opera. It
has been said that for 'Dido and Aeneas' there
were no precedents, and that its composition at
that moment was a freak of nature or at least an
experiment. Masterpiece as 'Dido' is, it is the
genius of the man and not the uniqueness of the
form that is surprising. Purcell had already
shown his ability to organise a sequence of movements into one continuous whole in his Odes,
anthems and dramatic scenes and the composition
of this little work for Mr. Priest's Academy at
Chelsea could have given him no trouble from
the purely formal point of view once the character
of the libretto was settled. In fact, it may be
said that it was the very nature of the performance
which gave to the opera many of the qualities for

[1] Compare also 'Lilliburlero,' described as 'a new Irish tune'
because it was associated with a pseudo-Irish political ballad.

which it has been most praised, its concentration, its directness, its swift and vivid presentment of the drama. Not less than any of Purcell's works 'Dido and Aeneas' was an occasional piece; written for schoolgirls, so that the chief parts are for soprano; designed for amateurs, so that the music is fairly simple in range and style; adapted to limited resources so that the instrumentation and stage-requirements are kept within modest limits; and since Mr. Priest was a successful teacher of dancing, freely interspersed with dances. In it Purcell invents no new form. The overture, the recitatives, ariosos, songs on a ground bass, choruses and instrumental interludes, had all been attempted before. We cannot trace anything tentative or experimental in the whole work. On the contrary it is the sureness of the strokes that constitutes its chief pride. For the echo chorus there were many precedents[1] and for the continuous form Blow's 'Venus and Adonis' a few years earlier supplied the model. The scenes are all very short and the whole work plays for something like an hour and a quarter. The style is variegated, like all Purcell's work, but

[1] A 'Fantasia in Echo' quoted by Parry (Oxford History of Music, Vol. 3, p. 312) published in 1603 by Banchieri contains an anticipation of the typical Purcell echo effect. Banister wrote an Echo song in Shadwell's version of 'The Tempest' which Pepys found 'mighty pretty.' The introduction of the Echo organ after the Restoration would explain Purcell's frequent adoption of the device.

that does not prevent it from having a dramatic consistency. It is full of personal mannerisms, yet nowhere did Purcell write with more spontaneous feeling. It is at once simple, sincere, unaffected, technically sophisticated and intensely human.

A fortunate conjunction of circumstances brought the work into being. The librettist was Nahum Tate, shortly afterwards to become Poet-Laureate. He was a poor and inept poet, as many grotesque lines in this opera prove. But in adapting, possibly with Purcell's aid, his earlier drama 'Brutus of Alba,' he proves himself to have had a considerable sense of the stage. 'Dido and Aeneas' is, indeed, a very skilful piece of dramatic work on a small scale. If it were not, even Purcell's genius would have failed to overcome the verbal insipidity of many of the individual passages. It is direct and there is scarcely a line of padding, no redundancy. Pitiful as poetry, it is quite excellent as a 'book' and why should it be judged on any other grounds? In the second place, there was the factor of the ballet-master, Josiah Priest. Priest was attached to the Dorset Gardens Theatre. He had been associated with Davenant's version of 'Macbeth' and he was later to be connected with the productions of 'King Arthur,' 'Dioclesian' and 'The Fairy Queen.' There is no doubt that he was the foremost English exponent of dancing of the day. Purcell's later works were deeply indebted to the introduction of stage-dancing in 'Dido and Aeneas.' The music of no composer has a finer quality of movement. Indeed it is tempting to claim for Purcell the title of the greatest master of musical gesture that has ever lived. To Priest Purcell's music must have owed a great deal, besides the chance that his invitation gave him to write an entirely operatic work. In 'Dido and Aeneas' he becomes aware for the first time of the full dramatic possibilities of self-contained instrumental music. Opera and ballet are closely allied, the more closely allied the better, for opera is drama in terms of music and music is in the final resort movement. The sacrificial scenes of Purcell's earlier stage efforts, useful enough as points of repose in the action and as excuses for extended choral developments, have the fatal defect as a basis of music-drama that they are static and impede the dramatic movement of the work. In such a school Purcell could never have learned to write a continuous opera and when he reverted to the professional stage, hidebound to the tradition that music should be invoked only for the purposes of pageantry, the outlandish or the supernatural, he had no chance to prove that music was capable of carrying through the whole of the dramatic action. But he had learned his lesson. He had learned how to write characteristic instrumental music and also vocal music, which, as we shall see, conjures up visions of stage-action.

The third factor in 'Dido and Aeneas' and the supreme one, is Purcell's own uncanny sense of dramatic characterisation. This is the clue, it need hardly be said, to the whole of his music, whether he is writing for a church, the platform or the stage. Under this aspect, and in the psychological truth of his music, there are only two other masters that can be placed in the same rank – Mozart and Wagner. It is absurd to represent Purcell as a pleasant little fresh-air composer. His music has the very odour of the theatre. It is immensely artificial; in other words, full of artifice. 'Dido' could not remain, what it undoubtedly is, the earliest example of a completely satisfying and dramatic opera, upon whose conventions time has had not the smallest effect, if it were not that it is conceived so intensely in terms of the stage, unhampered by literary or musical theories, devoted quite simply to the practical purpose, and undeviating in its regard for the immediate effect. It came about almost by accident – the English have no talent for working to an artistic theory. It probably seemed quite unimportant at the time and there is no evidence that, after its single performance, it was ever staged for the next two hundred years. Purcell seems to have had no idea that he was making any contribution to that problematical hypothesis, the future of English opera. He simply made a little work for an end-of-term function, and as the young ladies were more gifted in singing, deportment and dancing than in dramatic interpretation, he and his collaborators cast the whole thing in the form of an opera which allowed for plenty of opportunities for the display of their special talents. The story was familiar; the text was simple and easily followed. The drama, with its motive of tragic love, was of the kind that might be expected to appeal to school-girls. Yet in a sense it was universal and it is the human qualities of 'Dido' that have kept it alive.

'Dido and Aeneas' has been so often discussed that there is little need to deal with it in detail here. The songs on ground basses are unforgetable. The vivid dialogue, the swift and dramatic recitatives, the lovely echo chorus 'In our deep vaulted cell,' the raciness of the sailor's scene, the weird atmosphere of the witches' episodes, the touching emotion of Dido's death song, so much enriched by the final chorus 'With drooping wings' – all is conceived with a perfect sense of dramatic fitness. Professor Dent has said that 'it conforms to no tradition; it has no sense of style,' whereas Mr. Gustav Holst has recognised in it the supreme essential of a unity of style. Style is a difficult matter and may be differently interpreted.[1] That it is a matter of mere thematic consistency or technical procedure pure and simple is a heresy derived from the modern use of leading themes. We can best define it in connection with dramatic works as the adoption of a fundamental tone which in spite of deviations for particular illustrative purposes yet governs the whole mood of the work. And such fundamental tone Purcell's 'Dido and Aeneas' has. It is swift, concise, vital and realistic, despite its romantic subject. There are no trimmings. Every stroke tells. And at the end there is a feeling of complete fulfilment. What more can we ask of a dramatic work?

Yet 'Dido and Aeneas' remains outside the category of Purcell's normal theatrical work. His excursion into the field of amateur opera was an isolated event. His main energies were devoted to a professional theatre with quite different ideals. It seems strange that his work in the latter

---

[1] Parry defines it as 'the consistent adaptation of the materials to the conditions of presentment.' Form, he says, is based on the same influences. Parry's criterion is that art must be above all efficient, well-organised – it is the English ethical view. But English art has rarely conformed to English prejudices and has often become highly efficient and at the same time tremendously disorganised. Witness the semi-operas of Purcell's day and the revues of our own.

field should be judged by its failure to conform with the example set by his single experiment in writing what is technically a perfect opera, but an opera for amateurs. There is no sign that he was aware of compromising his art in any way by associating it with the current English compromise of the semi-opera. He was sufficiently the man of the hour to have insisted on his method, had he possessed any theories as to the nature of opera. But when it is regretted that Purcell never followed up the precedent of 'Dido and Aeneas,' it remains to be proved that he had the smallest perception of the fact that he had done anything out of the way, or that the particular form he adopted was superior to the type of work to which he devoted his main energies during the brief years to come.

Chapter III

MUSIC AND SPECTACLE

SO far we have seen Purcell mainly under the aspect of a court and church composer, writing his occasional odes and equally occasional anthems and making brief and somewhat unprofitable excursions into the domain of theatre-music. That he produced, incidentally, a masterpiece in 'Dido and Aeneas,' was no more than a stroke of chance, though not in the sense that there was anything freakish or inexplicable in the music. Simply, it lay outside his official routine and it had not, nor could it have, any place on the professional stage of that time.

He was now thirty and for the remaining six years of his life the theatre was to claim his chief attention. During these years (1690–95) he wrote music for over forty plays, of which six demand more than passing notice as constituting in the main the type of dramatic opera which was the particular convention of the Restoration period. The six works are 'Dioclesian,' 'King Arthur,' 'The Fairy Queen,' 'Bonduca,' 'The

Tempest' and 'The Indian Queen.' In them all his virtues are summed up, all his powers reach fulfilment. He begins and ends as a dramatic composer but it is only in these last years that he finds his most congenial sphere of activity. Had he at the same time had the good fortune to discover a Quinault,[1] he might have given the world a series of masterworks which would have eclipsed the entire operatic output of the 17th century. He had greater gifts than any of his contemporaries, not even excepting Alessandro Scarlatti, who was born in the same year as Purcell though he lived thirty years longer. Scarlatti is no doubt a more notable example in musical history both as a force and as the originator of a tradition. Purcell created no example, established no tradition. Handel certainly took many things from him but he was in no sense his successor. Indeed, in so far as Handel touched English music in its most vital form, he virtually undid, in his oratorios, the whole of Purcell's work in the setting of the English language.

The stage for which Purcell wrote has generally been set down as a trivial and licentious one, and his music has suffered under the imputation of being associated with plays which are for the most part dead and for the rest nowadays impracticable. This is a very partial view of the

[1] Lully's librettist.

case. Modern investigation has done much to lighten the burden of these charges and the possibility of a renewal of life in many works which have fallen under the lash of the moralists and literary historians, who have regarded the printed page rather than the theatrical milieu to which they belong, is not so remote as it once seemed. The rehabilitation of the period, so long under a cloud, has proceeded apace in recent years, but so far it has scarcely touched the work of its leading musical figure. Indeed those who have done most to restore Purcell's good name, have usually ended by throwing up their hands in despair at his impracticability.

No critics of the Restoration theatre were more severe than the writers who were contemporary with it. They heaped satire and burlesque upon the heroic plays and spectacular musical dramas of the day, but they failed to stay their progress. Beside the deadly shafts of the Duke of Buckingham and the squibs of the farce-writer Duffett, the moralistic out-pourings of Jeremy Collier seem mere humourless travesties. What is certain is that it was a period of immense theatrical activity. The stage had recently been released from the Puritan ban. It was an experimental stage, not a little devoted to the exploitation of new scenic devices. It was served by some of the greatest actors in English dramatic history and by singers, who, even if they were not great, were at least enormously applauded. It was not a little devoted to adaptations, though no more so than the stage of our own time, and it was supported by a public that demanded novelty at every turn, and if not novelty, then the repetition of its favourite sensations. It was a stage eminently favourable to the realisation of an intimate partnership between music and drama. Yet the partnership was rarely consolidated on terms of equality. The musician remained on the whole the bond-servant of the drama and only the genius of a Purcell raised him, on rare occasions, to the dignity of a free individual.

Purcell seems to have cheerfully accepted the responsibility of doing what was required of him. At the height of his powers he wrote nothing that was not commissioned, unless we place the second set of sonatas and some of the harpsichord pieces late in his career. Immense as was his industry in these last few years, it was not as great as it may seem on paper. To many of the plays for which he wrote the music, he contributed no more than a song or two and a few act-tunes. We can still remain amazed at his fertility, without feeling, except on very rare occasions, that he overtaxed his resources or produced merely perfunctory work. There was every temptation to him to give the public what it wanted, but he hardly ever relaxes his musicianship or departs from his own standard of craftsmanship. No doubt in many of his incidental songs and musical numbers he relies somewhat freely on his chosen formula. The words, were in truth, often appallingly conventional and the ubiquitous Celia with her 'thousand charms,' or some other colourless nymph, was scarcely calculated to inspire him with music of very profound import. We see him, the greatest composer of the day, writing its shop-ballads and theatre-ditties, its mad-scenes and conventional pastorals, putting his hand to the risky Dialogues between wives and husbands, and doing it with an obvious gusto. The introduction of a musical number by Mr. Henry Purcell was a feature on which the managers came increasingly to rely. There was scarcely ever more than a pretence that the thing was dramatically appropriate and with the usual 'Come, a song' or 'Strike up, boys,' the play was held up while the characters (nominally) but the house (more particularly) were entertained with a song and dance. Sometimes, but rarely, the introduction of music is dramatically appropriate, as in the serenading scene in Dryden's 'Amphitryon,' where Jupiter 'signs to the musicians, Song and Dance; after which Alcmena withdraws, frowning.' More often the song is introduced with some such lines as 'Come up, Gentlefolks, from below; and sing me a Pastoral

Dialogue, where the Woman may have the better of the Man, as we always have in Love matters.' Or, as in 'Bonduca' it is used for purposes of atmosphere:

> Lucius, I'd have the song you taught me last.
> I fear I do resemble now the swan
> That sings before its Death.

The old tradition of the use of music for scenes of supernaturalism survives. 'At the end of the song, a dance of spirits. After which, Amariel, the guardian Angel of St. Catharine descends to soft musick with a flaming sword. The spirits crawl off the Stage amazedly and Damilcar runs to a corner of it' (Dryden's 'Tyrannick Love'). These stage directions show how completely the dramatists were enamoured of stage effect. They are all written, as it were, from behind the curtain, rather than from the angle of dramatic truth. The dramatists liked, no doubt, to feel that they were stage-managing their own plays. But at least it proves that they thought in terms of the theatre, and not of literary effect. Whether the producers followed their instructions or whether their published directions were written after the rehearsals, is more problematical.

Many of the works for which Purcell wrote music began life as straight plays. At their revival, excuses were found for the introduction of a little music, the usual 'song and dance.' The theatrical public of Purcell's day was very much like our own. It would not support opera, but it liked to have some ear-tickling musical episodes introduced from time to time into its dramatic entertainments. It did not much matter if the music was dramatically irrelevant so long as there was a chance of hearing some popular stage figure, such as Jemmy Bowen or Miss Cross, (familiarly known as 'the Boy' and 'the Girl'). Into plays based on foreign subjects, such as D'Urfey's 'Don Quixote,' totally inappropriate songs such as Purcell's 'Genius of England' would be introduced by way of incidental entertainment. By the time we reach Congreve's play 'The Old Bachelor' (1692) the tradition is so well established that the dramatist himself could cause one of the characters to say 'Pray oblige us with the last new song.' The type of song usually deals cynically or knowingly with the casuistry of love. Sometimes the managers would economise by adapting new words to a tune which had already caught the public fancy or Purcell himself would save time by utilising the music of a successful song for an instrumental act-tune in a later play. Thus, the delicious little song, 'There's not a swain on the plain' in 'Rule a wife and have a wife' is a very clever adaptation of words to a hornpipe in the 'Fairy Queen' produced a year earlier; and the instrumental 'song-tune' in the 'Virtuous Wife' is identical with the song 'Ah, how sweet it is to love' in Dryden's 'Tyrannick Love.'

The amazing thing is that Purcell, under these conditions, should have turned out so much music that is of permanent value. His entr'acte music is unsurpassed for theatrical atmosphere. From the time of Shakespeare the music had traditionally formed part of the stage-properties, either as a behind-scene flourish or as the on-stage accompaniment to a song. In Shadwell's 'Tempest' the musicians for the first time, apparently, leave the obscurity of the stage-gallery and come out into the open as an orchestra, conventionally placed in front of the stage. This was, for the time, a great step forward, from the point of view of music drama. It meant that in the perspective of the entertainment music was no longer a mysterious agency introduced from behind scenes, and confined in its operations to the effect it might have on the persons in the drama, but was recognised as a factor in the presentment of the dramatic idea. But English mentality appears to have been unable to accept the full implications of the precedent. It clung to the superstition that music was chiefly to be invoked for scenes of ritual, pageantry or ceremony, and, if not, that it was to be a frank intrusion addressed, upon the

flimsiest excuse, to the audience as a concert-item.
In either case, it did not carry forward the drama.
It merely provided a halt, a point of repose, and
as soon as it was over, the action was to be resumed by means of the spoken word. So long as
the convention of recitative, which in Italian
opera was the carrier of the drama, remained
repugnant to English audiences, so long anything
in the nature of opera as understood abroad was
impossible. That this was a conscious motive in
the production of the typically English form of
the dramatic or semi-opera is probably untrue.
The stage was dominated by actors who were not
singers and who wanted to act. But conscious
artistic motives have never been the strong point of
English art, and the English form of the play with
music came about, as most English art-forms have
come about, from practical necessities. The public
wanted music; therefore music had to be introduced. But the actors wanted to speak and act;
therefore they were not to be replaced by singers,
who could perhaps sing, but could not act (there
seem to have been some exceptions, such as Mrs.
Bracegirdle, but in the main the two types were
kept in distinct categories). After all, it is not so
fantastic. The absurdities of operatic acting are to
this day a byword. The practical English compromise divided acting from singing and invented
a type of work that was foreign to the more

consistent form of opera that was being developed in Italy and France.[1]

English opera of the Restoration period was in the very least degree the product of an artistic theory, as had been the Italian. It was brought on the stage partly in emulation of the new scenic devices that were being exploited abroad and partly to accommodate the new taste for public music. It was even more of an accident than a compromise. The theatrical interests of the time were turning in the direction of spectacular entertainments. It is usually a sign of decadence in the drama. But the complete change of outlook that had come over the theatre between the decay of the poetic drama and the rise of the heroic play in a large measure accounts for the type of work presented. Stage-machinery was a comparative novelty and it was soon developed to a point that seems incredible even to us, who are accustomed to the scenic splendours of the modern stage. Reading some of the bizarre stage-directions with which these works are so liberally sprinkled, we can scarcely wonder that the novelty of the sensations

---

[1] Bishop Sprat, the first historian of the Royal Society, replying to the French observer Sorbière, who visited England in 1663, contrasts the French and English stages. 'The French,' he says, 'for the most part take only one or two great men and chiefly insist upon some one remarkable accident of their story. . . . The English on their side make their chief plot to consist in a greater variety of actions and besides the main design, add many little contrivances.'

caught the public fancy, or that flying witches, capering demons and gods and goddesses descending from the machine tended to oust the more serious type of play. Dryden seems to have reconciled himself to the fact that in opera it was the music and the spectacle that counted – 'these sorts of entertainment,' as he said, 'are principally designed for the Ear and the Eye.' That the result was, except occasionally, a work of art, cannot be alleged, but that it was often a highly successful theatrical entertainment can hardly be denied. We are absolved from the responsibility of regarding as an artistic product a practical expedient that was governed by the theatrical conditions of the time.

A line may, however, be drawn between the plays in which Purcell was merely an incidental composer and those in which his music was the predominant factor – those, in short which merit the name of dramatic operas. In the majority of the plays for which he wrote music during the last six years of his life, the connection was no more than casual. There was normally a theatre band of strings available, and an overture and some act-tunes were all that was required with perhaps a song or two introduced, by hook or crook, into the action. Many of these plays, such as D'Urfey's popular burlesque on the subject of 'Don Quixote' which ran into a second and third part before the

public tired of the subject, were the fruit of collaboration, very much in the spirit of the modern
musical plays and revues, the only difference being that the composers engaged were genuine
composers, 'the most Eminent Masters of the Age'
as they were claimed to be – it was scarcely an
exaggeration in many cases. Towards the end of
his life, it is clear that Purcell began to dominate
the theatre as he already dominated the church
and the assembly, and it was the growing recognition of his greatness as an artist, or if not that, his
success with the public, that led to his constant
employment. The run of plays at the time was
not lengthy, as we understand the matter. Ten
or twelve days constituted an average success,
though as Downes tells us, the cost of mounting
these productions was often so heavy that the company profited little. Purcell's forty-four plays in
the course of six years is enough to indicate his
position in the theatrical world. Revivals were
frequent and occasions would be seized for writing new musical settings, as well as the re-
arrangements of the text and scenes. It is a precedent which makes some of these works more
feasible to-day than they may seem at first sight,
more so, indeed, than many self-contained operas
that are irrevocably dated. Samuel Butler's criterion that if a work of art is to be considered at
all, it must be considered as existing in the state in

which it was first produced, scarcely applies here, for these pieces were not works of art. There is a supreme lack of style about them, except in so far as Purcell's music lends style to the sung passages. If they are ever to be revived and adapted to modern conditions, it can only be through meting out to them the same kind of treatment that they received in their own day.

Before turning to the major works in which he was concerned, we may glance at some of the general features of Purcell's incidental music. The overtures are often identical in form with those of the church anthems, that is a stately prelude followed by a more or less developed fugal movement in a livelier style and in triple time. Purcell shows great affection for carrying the same rhythmic figure throughout a whole movement and some of his overtures are brilliantly effective studies in persistent figure. The act-tunes and dances consist of airs, minuets, sarabands, bourrées, and above all hornpipes. He has comparatively few jigs but his innumerable hornpipes are among his most characteristic and infinitely variable measures. Purcell imparts every subtlety of rhythmic inflexion to these movements, which are capable of extension or contraction according to his fancy. They are in triple time and quite different in spirit from the common-time hornpipes which later became associated with sailors' dancing. These movements are invariably short but they contain much sparkling music. They have no particular relevance to the play in hand and might equally well be transferred from one to another. But they are excellent theatre-music and despite their similarity of form, Purcell's copiousness of melodic invention is scarcely anywhere seen to better purpose. That a string of them makes a suite of a rather miniature kind is true, but as ballet-music they are incomparable. Purcell's sense of movement, of gesture, is supreme. The music of few composers so much invites the accompaniment of action.

The songs are often conventional in sentiment. The appearance of the coy and cruel nymph and the lamenting swain and all the apparatus of the pastoral tradition, is a trifle monotonous. But individually the songs are of an extraordinary range and variety considering the frequency with which the same sentiments call for expression. Purcell's tendency in later years was increasingly towards the more florid Italian style but he can always turn out the racy type of colloquial song where the words have any pith or point. He develops the refrain-song in Rondo-form, of which 'Lucinda is bewitching fair' in 'Abdelazer' is a good example and 'I attempt from Love's sickness to fly,' the best known. The adjective that typifies (and damns) so many of the verses of a period is 'charming.' It seems to be the height of the poetic ideal and it led Purcell into many pages of conventional work which is in truth no better than the cliché-ridden formulas of the ballads of later times. But Purcell frequently saves an otherwise conventional song by the vigour of his handling of the bass, and occasionally, however stereotyped the words may be, he can bring off a brilliant effect, as in 'I see she flies me' (Aurengzebe) with its racing bass figure imitated by the voice and inverted with great skill at the change of sentiment to the lover's 'despair.' The peculiarity of many of these songs is that while the sentiment is more often appropriate to the male sex, the chosen voice is apparently the soprano. Even in the plays in which the music is a more integral feature, the songs are frequently given to a voice that seems to us inappropriate, though such songs as the well-known 'What shall I do to show how much I love her?' in 'Dioclesian' were no doubt presented to the accompaniment of some action or pose by the appropriate figures.

Many of the musical interludes, such as the popular duets and dialogues were frankly entertainments introduced for the diversion of the spectators. There is the delicious duet for a clown and his wife ('Since times are so bad') in the second part of 'Don Quixote,' a typically Purcellian running six-four movement. The tone of

the more common duets in which the man tempts
the maid is often a trifle insipid but as sung by the
popular figures of the Boy and the Girl, no doubt
they were relished by contemporary audiences.
There is a lively Pastoral Dialogue in 'Amphitryon' full of pleasant conceits, but on the whole
it is the humorous duets that represent Purcell in
his most spontaneous mood. The scenas and mad
songs have already been noticed. These contain
some of Purcell's most ambitious efforts. The bass
songs such as 'Let the dreadful Engines' ('Don
Quixote,' Part I) are particularly notable. Above
all Purcell is never so happy as when setting his
impertinent little love-songs, with their slightly
indiscreet words, such as those for the soprano in
'The Fatal Marriage' and 'The Mock Marriage.'
'Nymphs and Shepherds' (from 'The Libertine')
and 'I attempt' ('Indian Queen') are no better
than a score of others, and indeed considering the
somewhat limited range of their poetic idea, Purcell's incidental songs are often astonishingly vital
and varied. In all this music it is comparatively
rarely that he sinks into the trivial and the uninspired and in almost every play there is something, an act-tune, an overture, a song, or a duet
that repays examination.

It was with the production in 1690 of 'Dioclesian,' Betterton's adaptation of Beaumont and
Fletcher's 'The Prophetess,' that Purcell entered

on the full tide of his public theatrical career. Betterton was in truth no poet, but he was the foremost actor-manager of the day and he knew what went well on the stage. It was Purcell's first chance of showing what he could do on a big dramatic scale. If 'Dido and Aeneas' had failed, from the circumstances of its production, to attract much public notice, 'Dioclesian' was a challenge that could not be overlooked. It was splendidly mounted and Purcell seems to have made as much haste as possible to get the music published. The score is one of the most ambitious he ever wrote (including flutes, three oboes – one tenor – bassoon and trumpets) and indeed there is more than a suggestion of deliberate technical virtuosity in it. The 'book' is marred by touches of a flat-footed pseudo-poetic style that is frequently little better than doggerel. But this is less material in view of the free musical treatment to which Purcell subjects the lines, breaking them up and repeating them at will. The most striking feature of the work is, indeed, the scale of the combined choral and instrumental episodes. These are three in number. The first is a triumphal scene in which the soldier Diocles is proclaimed Emperor after achieving a stroke of political vengeance. This is ushered in, like so many of Purcell's ceremonial scenes, with a bass solo and a chorus 'Great Diocles the Boar has Killed.' There is some typical word-painting. The chorus interjects short phrases in an effectively exultant mood, and the temper of the music changes with every new suggestion of the words. Purcell then proceeds to build up the scene by way of solos, duets and choruses, varying the instrumental colouring but keeping before us from time to time the general mood of rejoicing, by means of trumpet airs and an exciting unaccompanied exclamation from the whole chorus 'Sound all your instruments,' followed by a flourish. The music is also held together by a recurrent movement which later appears as an act-tune, and is almost like a leit-motiv. A short intervention due to the supernatural agencies of the prophetess, Delphia, leads somewhat incongruously to a 'Dance of Furies' – the mixture of pageantry, heroics, supernaturalism, comedy and ballet-spectacle in this work fully merit the contemporary Sorbière's description of the English preference for hotch-potch – and the act closes with the chorus-tune which has already been largely used. The music is unequal, but at least it has a sense of theatrical effect, both in the variety of the choral sections, the use of pauses, the instrumental interludes and the general sense of crowd-gesture.

The choral scene in the fourth act is less extended. The fame of Dioclesian is again celebrated in 'artful numbers and well-chosen verse' (alleged). What gives the scene its chief interest is the elaborate finale worked out to an imposing climax. But the really memorable feature of 'Dioclesian,' apart from some descriptive dances, in which Purcell and the ballet-master Priest again found themselves in association, is the superb inspiration of the final Masque, dramatically a quite irrelevant episode but fortunately self-contained and capable of being detached. Not even in 'The Fairy Queen' does Purcell give us such a breathless succession of beautiful numbers, perfectly characterised. The Act in which the Masque occurs opens with a country dance, one of the rare examples in Purcell of his deliberately adopting a folk style – the modal inflexion of this exquisite little air and Purcell's choice of this type of measure to introduce a pastoral scene are characteristically well judged (small matter that the scene happens to be placed in rustic Italy).

In the Masque itself, he draws on such dances as the Paspe and the Canaries and writes others of his own that are equally engaging. The rhythmic variety of Purcell is one of his greatest assets as a stage composer. Indeed he is not less adventurous in this respect than in his bold harmonic strokes. He seems incapable of monotony. As an entertainment the Masque is the best thing in the work. The opening chorus with the phrases given out singly by the soprano and

echoed dramatically by the chorus-singers, presumably behind scenes, is a fine prelude and the
whole sequence of solos, duets, choruses and
dances is inspired with a fantasy, humour and a
vitality that Purcell rarely excelled. It is not so
much that the musical quality is exceptional
though several of the choral numbers are splendidly spacious, as that the absolute aptness and
dramatic integrity of the chosen style of each
number gives the work an extraordinary conviction. Movement and gesture are expressed in
almost every line and if facial expression could be
conveyed in music, Purcell's music would convey
it.

'Dioclesian' and his own 'Amphitryon' in the
same year were the means of bringing Dryden
over to Purcell's side and the result was their collaboration in the patriotic spectacle of 'King
Arthur.' The play has been severely disparaged,
though Mr. Montague Summers finds it 'a delight-
fully rococo fantasy' and declares his conviction
that it is 'the only English play, upon this legend,
of poetic value.' From the musical point of view
(and, as it was written definitely as a dramatic
opera and not a play to be read for its absolute
poetic qualities, there is no reason why it should
be considered from any other angle) it has copious
merits. There are flatnesses, as we have noticed,
and something of that peculiar lack of spiritual

warmth which characterised so much of the verse of the Restoration period. Such lines as:

> Honour prizing,
> Death despising,
> Fame acquiring,
> By expiring.

ought never to have come from Dryden. But he seems to have written under the constraint of a feeling that verse intended for music was *sui generis* and that procedures which would be intolerable in spoken poetry were rightly to be adopted when the end in view was a musical setting. The actual play is a rather cumbrous and involved mixture of heroic bombast, pastoral entertainment, magical intrigue, sacrificial episode and masque-spectacle. It was in fact a typically English evasion of the operatic idea, with the actors on one side and the singers on the other, each making the most of their respective opportunities. That it was not an impracticable proposition is proved by its quite respectable theatrical history from the time of Purcell to that of Macready.[1]

Dryden in the prologue complains that authors were compelled to write down to the level of the audience's intelligence, but there is no suggestion

[1] It was revived by Garrick, Kemble, Siddons and Macready, people not likely to be concerned in theatrical impossibilities. In modern times it has been performed at Cambridge (1928). In spite of its lavishness Downes says that it was 'very gainful to the company.'

in Purcell's music that he found it necessary to write down to the level of their musical intelligence. Indeed the quality that distinguishes 'King Arthur' is the almost consistent adoption of the finest ideals of musical craftsmanship. It is perhaps Purcell's most notable dramatic achievement on the purely musical plane. The sheer tunes are of unsurpassed beauty. 'How blest are shepherds.' 'Come if you dare,' 'Two daughters of this aged stream,' and 'Fairest Isle' are enshrined among the immortalities of music.[1] The typically Purcellian touch, even if we may concede that it does not cover the whole of Purcell, is nowhere so much in evidence. The pastoral tunes, the sturdy choruses, the three-four measures with their varying accents, the dramatic declamation, the racy word-setting, the consummate use of descriptive device as in the celebrated 'Frost Scene' – all are here. Yet it is possible to feel that the real glories of 'King Arthur' lie in the brilliant illustrative use of purely formal methods such as the canonic echoes in 'Hither this way' and ' Come follow me,' the technical mastery of the 'Passacaglia' which moves with perfect ease amid its self-imposed restrictions and the daring of the choral writing. Purcell was capable of making demands on a theatre-chorus which would be

[1] Dr. Burney made his best remark apropos of this last song: 'This is one of the few airs time has not power to injure. It is of all ages and countries.'

accounted severe if they were offered to a choir
provided with copies. It is the consistently high
level of sheer musical interest that makes 'King
Arthur' one of Purcell's most fascinating works.
We expect works written for the stage to exhibit
on paper a certain thinness of musical effect.
The simplifications and broad effects of dramatic
music cannot as a rule be considered quite in the
same light as the procedures of absolute music, but
Purcell's music in 'King Arthur' can be examined
for its own sake and no apology need be made
for it.

Purcell seems to have dealt somewhat freely
with Dryden's libretto. He cuts several passages
which are redundant or unsuited to music. He
substitutes ensemble movements for solos, introduces dances, builds up a climax. When Dryden
writes a flat line (as 'Trust me, I am no malicious
fiend') Purcell blandly omits it. There are
several whole stanzas for which no settings appear
to have been made. The musician, provided that
he knows his business, is often surer in his instinct
for what is theatrically effective than the librettist, for the simple reason that he is bound by the
very nature of his medium to think in terms of
actual performance. Dryden was a practical man
of the theatre, but he was first of all a literary
craftsman and his uneasiness under the con-
straints of a medium so arbitrary as music, is all

too obvious. Nevertheless, 'King Arthur' was the best text that Purcell ever had given to him, and it is the only one that was designed at the outset as a complete dramatic opera. The fact that it inspired Purcell with some of his most consistently beautiful music in a style that is perhaps more homogeneous than that of any of his semi-operas, is a sufficient compliment to its practical virtues.

The overture is one of his most dramatic and psychologically truthful efforts in this kind. It is clearly a prelude to the clash of arms between the Saxons and Britons which is the main motive of the play, and indeed foreshadows some of the features of the opening sacrificial scene in the Saxon camp. This, as usual, begins, after the instrumental prelude, with a bass solo invoking the pagan gods, and the chorus interjects short phrases of a responsory nature. The scene develops into a fine series of choruses of an elaborate texture. The battle which follows is short and decisive; there are behind-scenes flourishes of trumpets and drums in Purcell's brilliant fanfare style; and then the conquering Britons enter with the martial song 'Come if you dare,' in strikingly different idiom to that of the Saxon choruses. In Act 2 the scene is concerned with the enchantments of the sorcerers and their spirits, who take part in the fortunes of the rival kings, Oswald and Arthur.

This is an opportunity for some deliciously airy music. Then follows a pastoral of no dramatic significance except as pure relief. In the next act comes the brilliant scene of the awakening of the Frost Genius, one of Purcell's most memorable passages of word and scene painting; later, a scene in which Arthur, in an enchanted wood, is beguiled by water-spirits and wood-nymphs, and finally a masque and various patriotic numbers in praise of England and St. George. The whole fantastic spectacle is typical of the post-Restoration love of supernaturalism combined with heroic action. As a convention it is no more preposterous than many things in romantic opera. Dryden's play utilised Purcell's powers in almost every direction. Many of the songs are of flawless beauty and the ensembles and instrumental music are perfectly stylised. 'King Arthur' is the most effortless music Purcell ever wrote.

'Bonduca,' though written four years later, may be considered here in view of a certain similarity of theme, though with the exception of one beautiful song, the music is practically confined to a single scene. The play is an adaptation of the tragedy by Beaumont and Fletcher dealing with the struggle of the Britons under Boadicea and, by an historical licence, also Caractacus, against the Romans. The temple scene is the most powerful and impressive of its kind to be found in Purcell.

Instead of being given to a single soloist, the invocations here are taken up in turn by four voices and immediately echoed by the chorus in imitation, with an effect of clamorous appeal. The second section is a fine piece of vigorous declamation sung by a Druid (bass) and calling on the gods of Britain to 'Check the tow'ring pride of Rome.' Then after a spoken passage follows a duet for two priestesses with the characteristic accompaniment of flutes and continuo, in praise of the pagan goddess with the chorus and strings taking up the refrain at the close. A short recitative and another duet 'To Arms' introduced by a trumpet obbligato in a still more bellicose tone, leads to the superb finale 'Britons strike home,' one of the things in Purcell that have never been lost sight of. The carefully balanced tonal scheme of the movements, the consistent energy of the writing, the passionate impulse of the whole episode are splendidly conceived. As operatic ritual it is magnificent. Verdi never wrote more vital music. Purcell has managed to colour the whole scene with a sort of barbaric splendour. He strikes, in the final chorus, a note of patriotic sentiment that is entirely unforced and which makes a tune like 'Rule Britannia' sound by comparison merely bumptiously chauvinistic.

What Purcell might have achieved, had he come into contact with poetry of a finer stamp than the majority of versifiers of his day were able to offer him, it is idle to speculate. With the exception of a few songs in the 'Tempest' he set nothing to Shakespeare's words, though he was, during these last years, associated on three occasions with plays which were derived from Shakespeare. The dramatist's works were not, indeed, neglected but the attentions they received from the adapters left little of the original inspiration of the poetry to be seized on by composers.[1] In point of fact, as modern English composers have found rather to their cost, Shakespeare is not in any sense a librettist. He is a self-contained playwright and any attempt to adapt his plays to musical purposes is bound to do violence to him in some shape or form. He had his own ideas of music as an accessory art and the opportunities for its introduction into his plays are strictly limited. Verdi could write two successful Shakespearean operas because in a foreign adaptation he was not hampered by comparisons with the original text. English composers are not so fortunate. Shakespearean adaptations are bound

---

[1] A classical instance of the peculiar perversions that were practised occurs in Davenant's adaptation of 'Macbeth.' Shakespeare has the lines:

> The Divell damme thee blacke, thou cream-fac'd Loone:
> Where got'st thou that Goose-looke.

Davenant's paraphrase is 'Now, Friend, what means thy change of Countenance.' (Hazleton Spenser, 'Shakespeare Improved.' 1927.)

to call up echoes of the original, at least among cultivated listeners.

The 'inimitable hand of Shakespeare' which Shadwell praises in his version of 'Timon of Athens' is not the least of the problems that beset the modern production of these works. If the adapters, instead of making the dramatist's works into 'plays' (as Shadwell sublimely claimed to have done) had made them frankly into operas, the task might be easier. Modern taste which does not shrink from tagged Shakespeare so long as it is sung, declines to accept tagged Shakespeare if it is to be spoken.[1] The adapters showed little courage in either direction. Shakespeare was not so transformed as to give his play an entirely new colouring and to bring it within the conventions of the period. He was merely meddled with. The sung portions, which are usually irrelevant masques introduced for the nominal entertainment of the characters, can only be retained as they stand, for the music has irrevocably fixed the text in its place. The dilemma is one which cannot be solved on any artistic grounds. But it is possible to make too much of the theoretical need for consistency of style. The tradition of pastiche in English stage entertainments has lasted down to our own day and it is as pastiche that Purcell's

[1] When Dryden asked Milton for permission to turn 'Paradise Lost' into an 'Opera,' Milton is said to have replied: 'Ay ! young man, you may tag my verses if you will.'

219

Shakespearean opera 'The Fairy Queen' must be considered. It at least has this advantage over works of art, that it can be re-fashioned to suit modern tastes in the same spirit that it was accommodated to the tastes of its own time.

'The Fairy Queen' was an adaptation of 'The Midsummer Night's Dream' by an anonymous hand. It was one of the most lavish productions of the time and its success was sufficiently extraordinary to call for a revival in the following year (1693) when a whole new musical scene was added and some further songs interpolated. If any one of Shakespeare's works is amenable to this kind of treatment, it must be granted that 'The Midsummer Night's Dream,' itself not a little of a pantomime, is the most likely example. Moreover the element of fantasy, the mixture of broad comedy, romantic enchantments and fairy nonsense, is so much in keeping with the spirit of opera as the period of Purcell understood it that it is only surprising that it did not receive the attention of the adapters earlier. The original play is considerably abridged to make way for the musical episodes and some of the scenes are telescoped. The chief characters are as in Shakespeare and the main action, apart from the comic scene of the drunken poet, is followed until Act 3 when Titania summons a 'Fairy Mask' for the enchantment of Bottom, and bids her fairies 'change this place to an enchanted lake.' This is the first of a series of spectacular transformations which give to the close of each act the character of a masque, culminating in the last act with the masque of Hymen in which the lovers are entertained with the fantastic appearance of a Chinese scene. Various songs and dances are rendered by the 'Chineses,' six monkeys are introduced in a comic dance, Hymen appears, and with various solos, duets, choruses and a final grand dance, the whole inconsequent Shakespearean pantomime comes to an end.

'The Fairy Queen' has generally been regarded as Purcell's stage-masterpiece and in the combination of dramatic vigour with which the various numbers are characterised, the picturesque aptness of the dance movements and the brilliant succession of vocal solos and ensembles, it deserves that title. It is the most fortunate of all his works in its setting and subject, the one which is richest in possibilities for the modern producer. The fairy music is as nimble-footed as a ballet by Morley. Mendelssohn's music to the same play is not inspired with more vivacity, sweetness and delicacy of touch. The instrumentation is varied and often strikingly original, as in the air of 'Night' with its three-part accompaniment of muted violins and violas. One of the most amusing of Purcell's Pastoral Dialogues occurs in the duet

between Corydon and Mopsa, while the scene of
the drunken poet tormented and pinched by the
fairies, with its stuttering word-setting and the
lurching gait of the poet's music shows Purcell's
genius for comic characterisation at its best. But
it is even more in his feeling for stage-movement
and stage atmosphere, as in the Sleep chorus and
the characterised dances, that 'The Fairy Queen'
is an advance on anything he had previously done.
Purcell was again working with Priest and the
dances he writes and the interludes for stage-
action, are strongly individualised. Instrumental
music plays quite a large part in the score, outside
the accompaniments of the vocal numbers, and the
dances were in fact specially praised at the time.
The solo songs such as 'Ye Gentle Spirits of the
Air,' 'When I have often Heard,' 'The Plaint,'
'Hark ! the Ech'ing Air,' are remarkably fresh
and varied and the pageant of the Four Seasons
contain some splendid choral work. The odd
thing is that although 'The Midsummer Night's
Dream' is itself comparatively rich in openings
for incidental music, Purcell was given no single
line of Shakespeare to set. But the fact is not
perhaps deeply regrettable. The poet's words
are merely the string on which the whole series of
musical, spectacular and choreographic episodes
are threaded. The spoken part, reduced to its
simplest elements, might indeed be regarded as

exercising a function similar to that of a 'narrator,' and used not to explain Shakespeare's plot in full but to mark its main bearings. Opera itself manages to succeed on a fairly limited amount of direct narration, and the music in 'The Fairy Queen' is sufficiently lengthy and important to warrant the treatment of the work as an opera rather than as a play.

With 'The Tempest' we are on rather more difficult ground. The treatment of Shakespeare was much more drastic and from that angle it is quite in line with the principles of operatic adaptation, but the music is far less extensive than that of 'The Fairy Queen,' and the respective proportions of spoken poetry and music are such that the work is bound to remain, in production, a play with music rather than a dramatic opera. The text which Purcell set was apparently a rehash of Shadwell's version of 1674 that has already been referred to in the first part of this book. Purcell was engaged, as so often, to make a new setting, for a revival, probably in the last year or two of his life. Apart from the overture, which is a long and well developed movement, his music does not begin until the third scene of Act 2 – 'A Wild island' where Alonzo, Antonio and Gonzalo are discovered. They are accosted by strange Devils who reproach and threaten them on account of their crimes. First comes a duet 'Where does the black Fiend Ambition reside?' for two basses, with some resemblance to the declamatory word-painting of the earlier anthems. Then a chorus adds a further menacing outburst:

> In Hell with flames they shall reign
> And for ever, for ever shall suffer the pain.

It is the setting and the association of the words 'shall reign for ever' that would make it a remarkable coincidence if Handel had never heard of this passage and perhaps unconsciously recalled it in the 'Hallelujah' chorus.[1]

Purcell's movement is in C minor, as befitting the dismal nature of the subject. The setting is brilliant and the subtleties of rhythmic accentuation at the words 'Care their minds unquiet will keep' are extraordinarily suggestive. The unfortunate wanderers have scarcely recovered from these visions when more apparitions appear and another demon calls up an array of spectral winds, in the terrific aria 'Arise ye Subterranean

[1] In the 'Dublin Courant' for 14–17 January, 1749, there was advertised a revival of 'The Tempest' with the original songs and music 'by the celebrated Purcell.' There were certainly earlier revivals. Handel was in Dublin in 1742 for the production of 'Messiah.'

Winds.' This is in Purcell's most daring bravura style. The dashing scale passages recall the 'Storm' music in 'King Arthur.' After this the Act ends with a ballet of winds.

In Act 3 we have the songs of Ariel, 'Come unto these yellow sands' and 'Full Fathom Five.' These are tantalisingly beautiful and Ferdinand is bewitched, as well he might be. They miss quite half of their effect, however, if sung as solos purely and simply. They are definitely songs with a chorus. The other two songs in this Act, 'Dry those eyes,' constructed on one of Purcell's most ingratiating bass melodies freely treated as a 'ground,' and 'Kind Fortune Smiles' which is of the type that is sometimes called Handelian, are equally lovely. In Act 4 there is a Dance of Devils all on a persistent dotted figure and Dorinda's air 'Dear Pretty Youth.' It is rather long-winded, like much of Purcell's later work, but it is vocally beautiful. In Act 5 occurs the masque of Neptune and Amphitrite with the ballet of Trytons which Prospero introduces with these very un-Shakespearean words:

> Now to make amends
> For the rough treatment you have found to-day,
> I'll entertain you with my magick Art:
> I'll, by my power, transform this place and call
> Up those that shall make good my promise to you.

The scene opens with a recitative and Air,

'Great Neptune', followed by the brilliant bravura air of Neptune himself (bass), 'Fair and Serene.' Neptune's songs are all on a big scale, with elaborate instrumental passages; so, too, are those of Aeolus, and several are constructed on a formal *da capo* plan. One of the best numbers is the delicious air of Amphitrite, 'Halcyon Days,' and Neptune's 'See, see the Heaven's smile,' with its captivating accompaniment, is equally good. The music of 'The Tempest' is amongst Purcell's latest and most ambitious works, so far as the actual span of the individual solos goes, and represents his mature art on its most formal and highly developed side. How far he might have travelled in this direction had he lived another twenty or thirty years and been further touched by Italian forces that were to influence Handel, is beyond calculation. There is a balanced logic and formality about some of the 'Tempest' airs, that seem to mark the beginning of a new phase. In 'The Indian Queen,' on the other hand, he seems to be reaching out to still further conquests in the direction of dramatic expression and to this, his last work for the theatre, we must turn for a final glance at his art.

'The Indian Queen,' by Dryden and Howard, is one of the most consistently dramatic works that Purcell came into touch with and is in many ways an epitome of all that he wrote for the theatre, with its scenes of ritual, its allegorical episodes, its swift dramatic declamation, its formal songs, and its instrumental numbers. The subject is magnificent, the fortunes of the adventurer Montezuma in the service first of the Ynca of Peru, and later of the usurping Mexican Queen, Zempoalla. Montezuma as a reward for his services to the Ynca has asked for the hand of his daughter, Orazia, and being refused, deserts to the other side. The Ynca and his daughter are taken prisoners. The son of Zempoalla, Acacis, meanwhile falls in love with Orazia, while Zempoalla conceives a passion for Montezuma. At this point occurs the first of the ritual scenes. Zempoalla has consulted the priest Ismeron on the subject of a dream. Ismeron proceeds to an incantation, the well known 'Ye twice ten hundred Deities.' The God of Dreams arises and discourages Ismeron's effort to know the future, whereupon Zempoalla falls into a melancholy humour. Ismeron tries to console her by calling up a vision of aerial spirits, who somewhat tactlessly sing of their happiness 'from human passions free' and the song 'I attempt from love's sickness to fly' follows with no better effect on the love-sick queen. Impatiently she dismisses Ismeron's conjuring tricks with the words:

> Death on these trifles. Cannot you find
> Some means to ease the Passion of my mind?

Ismeron mildly expostulates, 'Great Queen . . .' but she sweeps him aside with a threat to burn all his temples unless he finds some charm to cause Montezuma to fall in love with her:

> Make him but burn for me in flames like mine
> Victims shall bleed and feasted Altars shine:
> If not –
> Down go your Temples and your Gods shall see
> They have small use of their Divinity.

In Act 4 Montezuma is in prison and failing to win his love, the bloodthirsty Zempoalla decides to sacrifice him to the Gods along with the other prisoners of war. The final act takes place in the Temple of the Sun 'all of gold and four Priests in habits of white and red Feathers, attending by a bloody altar, as ready for sacrifice.' The Ynca, Orazia and Montezuma are brought in bound. Acacis interrupts the sacrifice in order to free Orazia, and is slain. Timely messengers arrive to announce that a revolution has broken out and that Montezuma has been proclaimed King. There is general confusion and in the violent scene that follows Zempoalla stabs herself. The Ynca is freed and Montezuma is united to Orazia.

Purcell's music is extensive. Besides the usual First and Second music which was played while the audience assembled, there is a strongly developed overture, the quick section of which is built on characteristically persistent rhythm and works up to an exciting climax. Purcell's grasp of the form of overture which he practised throughout his life continuously strengthened, and some of his later essays are inspired with fine dramatic feeling as well as being more clearly and firmly designed. After the overture there is a Prologue which, somewhat unusually, Purcell has set to music. It takes the form of a dialogue between an Indian Boy and Girl (Quevira) who at the rise of the curtain are discovered sleeping under the Plantain-Trees. There is a short trumpet flourish and the Boy awakes and calls upon Quevira to fly:

> By ancient prophecies we have been told
> Our world shall be subdued by one more old
> And see that world already's hither come.

As an idyllic prelude to the violent drama which is to follow this could be made quite effective. The boy's first solo is very elaborate but has at the same time a certain innocence of effect. The girl replies in an even more naïvely characterised air, 'Why should men quarrel here?' and finally the two join in a duet.

The first Act is all spoken. Act 2 is preceded by a striking symphony and contains what seems to be a short masque designed no doubt to console the love-lorn queen who 'appears seated upon a throne, frowning upon her attendants.' A figure

described as Fame enters with a train of followers
and sings Zempoalla's praises. This is taken up
by the chorus. Immediately afterwards Envy,
another symbolic figure, retorts upon these out-
bursts in a curious strain:

> What flattering noise is this,
> At which my snakes all hiss ?

And on the last note of each phrase, the followers
of Envy interject the single word 'hiss,' to coincide with the soloist's 'hiss' and 'this,' an amusing
piece of realism. There is next a short dialogue
between Fame and Envy, the latter declaring that
he will 'fly from the place where flattery reigns.'
Then after a repetition of the hissing song, Fame
bids Envy begone, the orchestra gives out the
strains of Fame's opening song which is sung in
chorus, and the scene concludes with a Dance.
The whole episode is irrelevant to the drama but
no more so than any episode in grand opera which
is introduced for diversion, such as a ballet.

Act 3 contains two of Purcell's most famous
songs. 'Ye twice ten hundred Deities' with the
air that follows is the dramatic incantation in
which Ismeron conjures up the God of Dreams.
It is a typical 'mood'-song, every phase of the
poem being illustrated by changes of mood in the
music. The God of Dreams replies in a lovely
solo with oboe accompaniment, 'Seek not to know

what must not be revealed.' The duet of the
aerial spirits 'How happy are we' which follows
after some spoken dialogue, is for alto and tenor
and then a chorus of spirits sings:

> Cease to languish then in vain
> Since never to be loved again.

After this comes the familiar 'I attempt from
love's sickness to fly' – lovely as a melody, if
scarcely calculated to soothe the already over-
wrought Zempoalla – and the scene ends with
spoken dialogue, as usual. The whole train of
movements though unsatisfactory from an operatic point of view, is enchanting in its musical interest, and a crowning beauty is the exquisite
little Rondo which serves as the Act-tune.

The final sacrificial scene, though not so extended as some of Purcell's other scenes of ritual,
is an extremely impressive example of his theatrical sense. It opens with an imposing chorus in
which the voices are skilfully disposed and answer
each other antiphonally. There is a short recitative by the High Priest to the words:

> You who at the altar stand
>   Waiting for the dread command;
> The fatal word
>   Shall soon be heard
> Answer, then, is all prepared?

And the chorus answers 'All's prepared.' Then
there is a solemn processional chorus which no

doubt was accompanied by some ritualistic hap-
penings on the stage, and the scene reverts to
spoken drama, ending in swift and sudden violence.

There is little cause to regret that Purcell did not
set the final Masque of Hymen, which was introduced to celebrate the nuptials of Montezuma
and Orazia. The dramatic significance of the
Masque is negligible and the play and its music
are already sufficiently long. Purcell died before
he was able to set this act, if he ever intended to do
so, and his young brother Daniel completed it in
a style that does credit to his respect for Purcell's
manner but is almost entirely devoid of inspiration.[1]

'The Indian Queen' might very well be added
to the list of Purcell's practicable stage works.
Musically it is on his very highest plane and the
drama itself has merits beyond many with which
he was associated. The problem of getting these
works on to the stage is, no doubt, a difficult one.
Their conventions are not our conventions and
they appeal in some respects to tastes that are no

[1] 'The Indian Queen,' however, seems to have been published
before Purcell died, for the score fell into the hands of unscrupulous parties, a certain May and Hudgebutt, who not merely
published it but addressed an impudent dedication to Purcell
himself, in which they pretend that his 'innate Modesty' would
not permit Purcell to patronise his own work, 'although in some
respects inimitable. But in regard that (the Press being now
open) anyone might print an imperfect Copy of these admirable
songs, or publish them in the nature of a Common Ballad, We
were so much the more emboldened to make this attempt, even
without acquainting you with our Design.'

longer current. But these adaptations are not incapable of being re-adapted, and the music alone in most cases would carry them through. Their absurdities of detail are no more pronounced than those of the average romantic opera of modern times and they are a good deal less obscure and far-fetched than many classical works in operatic history. Spectacle is of all forms of entertainment the one which wears the least well, for every age has its own ideas of the spectacular. But in an age which shows a devotion to spectacle and to revivals, at least as marked as that of the Restoration period, it should not be impossible for the imagination of a popular producer to be caught by such a fantasy as 'The Fairy Queen' and with a precedent of that sort established the music of Purcell might once more find its proper place in the public theatres.

For Purcell is, in the last resort, a man of the theatre. Take away the stage and nine-tenths of what is valuable in his music is lost. This does not mean that his dramatic music cannot be examined on its merits. On the contrary, there are few things more surprising in the whole of his immense output for the theatre than the general consistency and integrity of his musical craftsmanship. He may here and there lack inspiration and write conventionally, though with his faculty for surprise there are few completely dull pages in his music. He may seem to compromise his art by setting it so often in association with work of meagre poetic substance. But he hardly ever compromises his own steadfast ideals of musical technique. His technical resource never fails, even when the fires of his inspiration burn somewhat low. It is not that he is in any way an inventor of forms – he invented little in that line and was singularly devoted throughout his life to his chosen media – but that he uses forms creatively and with unfailing aptness. His instinct for choosing the right mould for his dramatic expressions is supreme. His conscious ideals may be accounted artistic rather by reason of their high technical aim than on account of any very lofty spiritual purpose. He gives no sign whatever of having had any clear perception of working towards an artistic goal and his whole development may seem at first sight to be nothing but a technical development. With such ideals he might have been nothing more than a seventeenth century Cherubini, writing his technically masterful, if poetically arid, works.

But Purcell happened to be at the same time a great dramatic poet and his steps were led, by a logical necessity, to the theatre, which occupied his main labours in the years of his full maturity. To throw over the whole of his dramatic music on the ground that it cannot be ever again put in its appropriate setting is a counsel of despair which means giving up most of what is still valuable in Purcell. These works are useless in the concert room. They cry aloud for movement, action, scene. They were written for a completely professional theatre with exclusively commercial ideals. That is why they should appeal to the professional theatre of our own time. For it is not true that the works of commerce are necessarily of low aesthetic vitality and that the works of 'art' are always of enduring interest, particularly in matters relating to the theatre. Indeed with the English ideal of art as the successful adaptation of means to ends, the kind of work that stands the best chance of being produced and even of surviving, is the outcome of practical necessity and feasible compromise. The semi-operas of Purcell are not, after all, so dead as the possibly more artistic works of Lully. Several of them have been revived, in whole or in part, in recent years, though only by the enthusiastic enterprise of amateurs. The amateur has often been able to drop a valuable hint to the professional and the suggestion that Purcell's stage-work is still capable of being produced is one of which the professional theatre is bound sooner or later to take notice.[1]

[1] Mr. C. B. Cochran some time ago announced a projected revival of 'The Fairy Queen' in conjunction with Mr. Gordon Craig. But nothing further has so far been heard of this interesting possibility.

EPILOGUE

'UNLUCKILY for Purcell,' exclaims Dr. Burney, 'he built his fame with such perishable materials that his works are daily diminishing . . . and so much is our great musician's celebrity already consigned to tradition that it will be as difficult to find his songs or at least to hear them, as those of his predecessors, Orpheus and Amphion.' But Purcell's fame, as soon as it ceased to be a contemporary memory and became part of the established musical belief which is so fatal in the long run to the reputation of any English composer, was built not so much on perishable as on partial materials, consisting of a slender proportion of his entire work and what is much more serious, of printed versions which did every kind of violence to his intentions.

Fatality has surrounded the publication of Purcell's music from the time of his own unsuccessful ventures down to the formation of the Purcell Society, over fifty years ago, when it was still possible to say that the majority of his works existed only in manuscript, and even if that reproach has now been to a large extent removed, it is very little to English credit that the Purcell

Society edition is still far short of completion. During the 18th century a certain number of Purcell collections were brought out but anything in the nature of a consistent attempt to publish his work languished for lack of support. The standard source of his songs was for long the not very skilfully edited 'Orpheus Britannicus,' published by his widow in 1698 and reaching a third edition in 1721. None of his larger choral or dramatic works saw light until a hundred years after his death, with the exception of the 'Te Deum and Jubilate' (1694), a few anthems and one or two of the Odes. A few of the better known dramatic numbers, such as 'Britons strike home' ('Bonduca'), 'Genius of England' ('Don Quixote'), 'From Rosy Bow'rs' (*ibid*), some patriotic pieces from 'King Arthur,' together with such things as 'Bess o' Bedlam' which ranked as 'celebrated old songs,' enjoyed a continuous popularity and fairly frequent calls for publication. The one side of his art which received the most consistent attention was, curiously enough, the one which for various reasons has been set rather low in the estimation of modern editors – the rounds and catches, 'pot-house effusions,' as Dr. Walker calls them. The disastrous methods of Boyce and the devoted, though not always scrupulous, work of Novello, in their editions of the church music seem to have inspired other editors with a passion for improving

Purcell, much in the same spirit that the Restoration dramatists sought to 'improve' Shakespeare. It is not merely that Purcell's harmonic licenses have had to suffer from being treated as faults of grammar, or the occasional aberrations of a man of genius which need correction, but that perfectly normal procedures have been tampered with by people with a mania for making 'arrangements.' Dr. Rimbault in the Musical Antiquarian Society's edition of 'Bonduca' noticed a case in which even so famous and straightforward a chorus as 'Britons strike home' was completely reharmonised.[1] The practice has unfortunately not altogether died out in our day, and it is still possible to meet with editions of Purcell's songs in which the bass has been unscrupulously altered and the harmonies emasculated.

As to performance, despite Dr. Burney, who was as usual exaggerating, the persistence of the Purcell tradition has been much more vital than is generally supposed. The vitality has perhaps been at low ebb from time to time and in the case of the church music it may be said that life has been prolonged notwithstanding a condition amounting to pernicious anaemia. By choosing the least interesting anthems and services and by adopting a style of singing that usually halves the intended pace, church choirs have managed to

[1] Alas, the Society's own editions were not beyond reproach.

238

prove that Purcell is one of the dullest composers of religious music that ever lived. Nevertheless, Purcell lives on even under these severe handicaps. As to his theatre-music, it may be doubted if any composer has ever been associated with works which have had a longer theatrical history than the majority of those for which he supplied the music. It has been so often reiterated that the music of Purcell is allied to works which had only an ephemeral interest that the plain facts of the matter have become obscured. It is not too much to say that every one of the plays for which Purcell wrote any considerable amount of music, with the possible exception of 'The Fairy Queen,' the most feasible of all, retained its popularity for the best part of the 18th century – that is, for a hundred years – and some, such as 'King Arthur' survived on the professional stage for a hundred and fifty years. Dryden's and Congreve's plays had a lengthy theatrical career and their revival in modern times has been in one or two instances accompanied by a revival of Purcell's music.

By a strange irony, it is only in our own day when his works have at length become in a large measure accessible through the medium of publication, that Purcell has suffered extreme neglect in the matter of performance. There is no department of music to which he did not contribute significant and entirely performable works –

perhaps there never was so performable a composer as Purcell. Yet there is no department of
music to-day in which he takes his place as
a matter of course in public performance. There
is no society, as there have been several in the
past, which is willing to devote itself to the study
and practice of his works – the Purcell Society
very early in its career abandoned the project of
performing him: a fact which rather seems to
prove that publication is not an unmixed blessing.
With the possible exception of 'Dido and Aeneas,'
no works of his are ever given except in an atmosphere which suggests that the interest is one of
curiosity, the museum-specimen view, and that
the justification is mainly educational or historical.
The result is that Purcell, the most professional
composer in English musical history, is totally
unknown to professionals, except in a few songs
and perhaps a keyboard piece or two, and is
generally regarded by them as a composer for
amateurs.

There is yet hope for Purcell. It is not an
entirely unprecedented phenomenon in musical
history for a composer to be set down in one period
as impracticable except for purposes of study, and
his music written off as being of only theoretical
interest, while at a later date he is made the
subject of a ritualistic worship under which every
note of his music has to be performed, the good

and the bad together. Such a composer is Bach. It is not an unheard of thing for a work which subsequently becomes one of the most popular in the repertoire to have passed through a period when it was presumed to be impossible of performance. It is within living memory that 'The Magic Flute' was considered to be a preposterous hotch-potch, the only redeeming feature of which was Mozart's music. For the rest it was not felt to be a work that goes well on the stage. We know that it is eminently practicable. It is not beyond the bounds of possibility that Purcell will one day be rediscovered in the way that Bach and Mozart have been rediscovered. What is certain is that in him this country made its biggest attempt to produce a complete composer, on the scale and of the scope of the half-dozen greatest composers in the world.

SHORT BIBLIOGRAPHY

In addition to the works mentioned below, acknowledgment is due to the various editors of the Purcell Society's volumes

Roger North, *Memoires of Musick* (Ed. E. F. Rimbault, 1846)

Roger North, *The Musicall Gramarian* (Ed. Hilda Andrews, 1925)

John Downes, *Roscius Anglicanus* (Ed. Montague Summers, 1928)

Anthony à Wood, *Life* (2 vols., 1772)

H. C. de la Fontaine, *The King's Musick* (1909)

A. Montague Summers, *Shakespeare Adaptations* (1922)

Allardyce Nicoll, *History of Restoration Drama* (1928)

J. S. Bumpus, *History of English Cathedral Music* (1908)

E. H. Fellowes, *The English Madrigal Composers* (1921)

Peter Warlock, *The English Ayre* (1926)

Edward J. Dent, *Foundations of English Opera* (1928)

H. C. Colles, *Voice and Verse* (1928)

William H. Cummings, *Henry Purcell* (Great Musician Series, 1881)

Dennis Arundell, *Henry Purcell* (1927)

INDEX

243

INDEX

244